In the Body of the World

IN
THE BODY
OF THE
WORLD

A MEMOIR

EVE
ENSLER

RANDOM HOUSE CANADA

PUBLISHED BY RANDOM HOUSE CANADA

www.randomhouse.ca

Library and Archives Canada Cataloguing in Publication

Ensler, Eve, 1953–
In the body of the world / Eve Ensler.

Issued also in electronic format.

ISBN 978-0-345-81323-7

1. Ensler, Eve, 1953–. 2. Authors, American—20th century—Biography. 3.
Cancer—Patients—United States—Biography. 4. Cancer patients' writings,
American. 5. Women human rights workers—Biography. 6. Women—Congo
(Democratic Republic)—Social conditions. I. Title.

PS3555.N75Z46 2013   812'.54   C2012-907993-6

Jacket design by Rodrigo Corral Design
Designed by Kelly Too

Printed and bound in the United States of America
1   3   5   7   9   10   8   6   4   2

For Toast, Lu, and
the women of the Congo

If you are divided from your body you are also divided from the body of the world, which then appears to be other than you or separate from you, rather than the living continuum to which you belong.

—Philip Shepherd, *New Self, New World*

SCANS

In the Body of the World

DIVIDED

A mother's body against a child's body makes a place. It says you are here. Without this body against your body there is no place. I envy people who miss their mother. Or miss a place or know something called home. The absence of a body against my body created a gap, a hole, a hunger. This hunger determined my life.

I have been exiled from my body. I was ejected at a very young age and I got lost. I did not have a baby. I have been afraid of trees. I have felt the Earth as my enemy. I did not live in the forests. I lived in the concrete city where I could not see the sky or sunset or stars. I moved at the pace of engines and it was faster than my own breath. I became a stranger to myself and to the rhythms of the Earth. I aggrandized my alien identity and wore black and felt superior. My body was a burden. I saw it as something that unfortunately had to be maintained. I had little patience for its needs.

The absence of a body against my body made attachment abstract. Made my own body dislocated and unable to rest or settle. A body pressed against your body is the beginning of nest. I grew up not in a home but in a kind of free fall of anger and violence that led to a life of constant movement, of leaving and falling. It is why at one point I couldn't stop drinking and fucking. Why I needed people to touch me all the time. It had less to do with sex than location. When you press against me, or put yourself inside me. When you hold me down or lift me up, when you lie on top of me and I can feel your weight, I exist. I am here.

For years I have been trying to find my way back to my body, and to the Earth. I guess you could say it has been a preoccupation. Although I have felt pleasure in both the Earth and my body, it has been more as a visitor than as an inhabitant. I have tried various routes to get back. Promiscuity, anorexia, performance art. I have spent time by the Adriatic and in the green Vermont mountains, but always I have felt estranged, just as I was estranged from my own mother. I was in awe of her beauty but could not find my way in. Her breasts were not the breasts that fed me. Everyone admired my mother in her tight tops and leggings, with her hair in a French twist, as she drove through our small rich town in her yellow convertible. One gawked at my mother. One desired my mother. And so I gawked and desired the Earth and my mother, and I despised my own body, which was not her body. My body that I had been forced to evacuate when my father invaded and then violated me. And so I lived as a breathless, rapacious machine programmed for striving and accomplishment. Because I did not, could not, inhabit my body or the Earth, I could not feel or know their pain. I could not intuit their unwillingness or refusals, and I most certainly never knew the boundaries of enough. I was driven. I called it working hard, being busy, on top of it, making things happen. But in fact, I could not stop. Stopping would mean experiencing separation, loss, tumbling into a suicidal dislocation.

As I had no reference point for my body, I began to ask other women about their bodies, in particular their vaginas (as I sensed vaginas were important). This led me to writing *The Vagina Monologues*, which then led me to talking incessantly and obsessively about vaginas. I did this in front of many strangers. As a result of me talking so much about vaginas, women started telling me stories about their bodies. I crisscrossed the Earth in planes, trains, and jeeps. I was hungry for the stories of other women who had experienced violence and suffering. These women and girls had also become exiled from their bodies and they, too, were desperate for a way home. I went to over sixty countries. I heard about women being molested in their beds, flogged in their burqas, acid-burned in their kitchens, left for dead in parking lots. I went to Jalalabad, Sarajevo, Alabama, Port-au-Prince, Peshawar, Pristina. I spent time in refugee camps, in burned-out buildings and backyards, in dark rooms where women whispered their stories by flashlight. Women showed me their ankle lashes and melted faces, the scars on their bodies from knives and burning cigarettes. Some could no longer walk or have sex. Some became quiet and disappeared. Others became driven machines like me.

Then I went somewhere else. I went outside what I thought I knew. I went to the Congo and I heard stories that shattered all the other stories. In 2007 I landed in Bukavu, Democratic Republic of Congo. I heard stories that got inside my body. I heard about a little girl who couldn't stop peeing on herself because huge men had shoved themselves inside her. I heard about an eighty-year-old woman whose legs were broken and torn out of their sockets when the soldiers pulled them over her head and raped her. There were thousands of these stories. The stories saturated my cells and nerves. I stopped sleeping. All the stories began to bleed together. The raping of the Earth. The pillaging of min-

erals. The destruction of vaginas. They were not separate from each other or from me.

In the Congo there has been a war raging for almost
thirteen years. Nearly eight million people have died
and hundreds of thousands of women have been
raped and tortured. It is an economic war fought over
minerals that belong to the Congolese but are pillaged
by the world. There are local and foreign militias from
Rwanda, Burundi, and Uganda. They enter villages and
they murder. They rape wives in front of their husbands.
They force the husbands and sons to rape their daugh-
ters and sisters. They shame and destroy families and
take over the villages and the mines. The minerals are
abundant in the Congo—tin, copper, gold, and coltain,
which are used in our iPhones and PlayStations and
computers.

Of course by the time I got to the Congo, I had
witnessed the epidemic of violence toward women
that scoured the planet, but the Congo was where I
witnessed the end of the body, the end of humanity,
the end of the world. Femicide, the systematic rape,
torture, and destruction of women and girls, was being
employed as a military/corporate tactic to secure
minerals. Thousands and thousands of women were
not only exiled from their bodies, but their bodies
and the functions and futures of their bodies were

rendered obsolete: wombs and vaginas permanently destroyed.

The Congo and the individual horror stories of her women consumed me. Here I began to see the future—a monstrous vision of global disassociation and greed that not only allowed but encouraged the eradication of the female species in pursuit of minerals and wealth. But I found something else here as well. Inside these stories of unspeakable violence, inside the women of the Congo, was a determination and a life force I had never witnessed. There was grace and gratitude, fierceness and readiness. Inside this world of atrocities and horror was a red-hot energy on the verge of being born. The women had hunger and dreams, demands and a vision. They conceived of a place, a concept, called City of Joy. It would be their sanctuary. It would be a place of safety, of healing, of gathering strength, of coming together, of releasing their pain and trauma. A place where they would declare their joy and power. A place where they would rise as leaders. I, along with my team and the board at V-Day, were committed to finding the resources and energy to help them build it. We would work with UNICEF to do the construction and then, after V-Day, would find the way to support it. The process of building was arduous and seemingly impossible—delayed by rain and lack of roads and electricity, corrupt building managers, poor oversight by

UNICEF, and rising prices. We were scheduled to open in May, but on March 17, 2010, they discovered a huge tumor in my uterus.

Cancer threw me through the window of my disassociation into the center of my body's crisis. The Congo threw me deep into the crisis of the world, and these two experiences merged as I faced the disease and what I felt was the beginning of the end.

Suddenly the cancer in me was the cancer that is everywhere. The cancer of cruelty, the cancer of greed, the cancer that gets inside people who live downstream from chemical plants, the cancer inside the lungs of coal miners. The cancer from the stress of not achieving enough, the cancer of buried trauma. The cancer that lives in caged chickens and oil-drenched fish. The cancer of carelessness. The cancer in fast-paced must-make-it-have-it-smoke-it-own-it formaldehydeasbestospesticideshairdyecigarettescellphonesnow. My body was no longer an abstraction. There were men cutting into it and tubes coming out of it and bags and catheters draining it and needles bruising it and making it bleed. I was blood and poop and pee and puss. I was burning and nauseous and feverish and weak. I was of the body, in the body. I was body. Body. Body. Body. Cancer, a disease of pathologically dividing cells, burned away the walls of my separateness and landed me in my body, just as the Congo landed me in the body of the world.

Cancer was an alchemist, an agent of change. Don't get me wrong. I am no apologist for cancer. I am fully aware of the agony of this disease. I appreciate every medical advance that has enabled me to be alive right now. I wake up every day and run my hand over my torso-length scar and am in awe that I had doctors and surgeons who were able to remove the disease from my body. I am humbled that I got to live where there are CAT scan machines and chemotherapy and that I had the money to pay for them through insurance. Absolutely none of these things are givens for most people in the world. I am particularly grateful for the women of the Congo whose strength, beauty, and joy in the midst of horror insisted I rise above my self-pity. I know their ongoing prayers also saved my life. I am in awe that it happens to be 2012, not twenty years ago even. I am gratefully aware that at just about any other point in history I would have been dead at fifty-seven.

In his book, *The Emperor of All Maladies*, Siddhartha Mukherjee says, "Science is often described as an interactive and cumulative process, a puzzle solved piece by piece with each piece contributing a few hazy pixels to a much larger picture." Science, then, is not unlike a

CAT scan, a three-dimensional magnetic electronic beam that captures images as it rotates around the body. Each image is separate but somehow the machine makes them seem like one.

This book is like a CAT scan—a roving examination—capturing images, experiences, ideas, and memories, all of which began in my body. Scanning is somehow the only way I could tell this story. Being cut open, catheterized, chemofied, drugged, pricked, punctured, probed, and ported made a traditional narrative impossible. Once you are diagnosed with cancer, time changes. It both speeds up insanely and stops altogether. It all happened fast. Seven months. Impressions. Scenes. Light beams. Scans.

THE BEGINNING OF THE END,
OR IN YOUR LIVER

Dr. Sean, who has a dour demeanor, holds up my CAT scan. It's suddenly my bad report card, my dirty underwear, a map of the Congo, and each potential tumor site is a mine. He holds it there and I wait for the pointer stick (he is already wearing the white coat). "Here—your body. As you can see, there appear to be masses in your uterus, your colon, your rectum. There is shadowing in various nodes and there is something in your liver." "Something?" I say. What something would be in my liver? A spoon? A poker chip? A parakeet? What could there be in my liver? "There are spots. They could be cysts. There are sometimes cysts on the liver." Ew, cysts on my liver. "There is definitely something there. We won't know 'til we are in there," he says. In there? In my liver? You won't know if I have cancer in my liver until you are in there? "And what

will you do if you find something?" I say. "We won't
know until we find it."

It is bad news. The worst news. This is the worst
day of my life. This is the day I am told I am going to die.
My heart is racing. I know liver. Liver is it. I am a recovering alcoholic. I lived with a many-times-recovering
alcoholic. He was one step away from cirrhosis. I know
about the liver. Once the liver goes, the whole story
goes. You can't live without a liver. But my liver would
have healed. I stopped drinking almost thirty-four
years ago. I quit smoking twenty years ago. I'm a vegetarian and an activist. I express my emotions a lot,
and I've had an incredible amount of sex. I lift weights
and walk everywhere, and it's in my liver. Oh my god,
it's in my liver.

Then a calm comes over me, the same calm that
used to descend as I approached a beating by my father.
I am calm. I am not panicked. I am going to die. This is
the beginning of the end. And I finally understand this
feeling I have had all year. Not depression, no, I have
not been depressed. This strange clarity/foreboding
that I would not live. So strong was this sense that I
talked about death all the time, reconciling myself to
it. "If I die on this trip, it will be okay," I would say. "I
have had a good life." I said this so often my son talked
to his shrink. He was worried. He wanted me not to

die and, more important, to stop talking as if I were about to die. The shrink said something about me being traumatized, depressed, and burned out by all the work I was doing in conflict zones. But I know things and I have sensed death in my body all year. I am not panicked and I am not even sorry for myself. Not at all. I have had an extraordinary life.

It is exactly the life I wanted. I have done what I wanted to do. I have seen the world. I have loved my son deeply, his children and my friends, and I have been loved. I wrote plays, and they meant things to some people, and I helped women, or I think I did. We leave the office and I hear myself calmly say to Toast, friend and assistant, intimate and manager, "I am going to the Congo tomorrow. I will need to let Mama C know when I am arriving." Toast looks at me like I am mad. "Excuse me?"

I say, "I am going to the Congo. The cancer is in my liver. You heard the doctor. You saw the CAT scan. Cancer in your liver means death. I need to see the women. I need to be with them in the Congo. I will be happy to die there." He says, "You are not going to the Congo. Your operation is in the morning. You need to be here. They will be operating on you." I say, "I am going," and he says, "You are not." "I am." "No, you're not." And it feels like we are yelling, but I am not sure we were yelling (Toast and I have never yelled in eight years), and it feels like we are wrestling but I don't think we were wrestling. "I am I am I am going to die in the Congo. I need to be there for the City of Joy. I made promises that I need to keep." He says, "They did not say it was definitely on your liver. They said they saw spots." "*Spots* is a euphemism, Toast. They couldn't say *tumor*. They couldn't say, 'We see hard lumpy cancer tumors on your liver.' They say *spots*. It is such a stupid word, *spots*. It makes you feel stupid just to say the word *spots*. Why couldn't they be forthright? Why couldn't they tell me the truth? I need the truth."

And we tumble out (not sure it was tumbling) into the hallway in the cancer building in cancer town, and we find two sickly-looking chairs, and we sit down and weep uncontrollably.

DR. DEB, OR CONGOCANCER

I had only met Dr. Deb on the phone. She was a voice, a surprisingly emotional doctor voice. At first it was a bit disconcerting. We have been taught for so long to expect our doctors to be distant and untouchable. The distance implies a certain training, a certain professionalism. They won't get lost in the mess of your bloody body or get drawn into your neurotic obsessing. We have been trained to believe this bifurcation of heart and head is necessary, something that will protect us, that embedded in this detachment is some magical shield that will keep us from the void. I know now that the opposite is true. The first time I talked to Dr. Deb, I didn't believe she was a doctor at the Mayo Clinic. She had called because she had been reading an article I had written about the atrocities and rapes happening to the women and girls in the Congo and she was crying on the phone. She could hardly speak through her tears. She was saying, "I will do anything to help. What can I do? What can we do to help?"

I think here is where I need to tell you about the Congo. It is hard to know where to begin. It is hard to know where anything begins—like the cancer itself. Was it the day I met Dr. Mukwege in New York City at NYU Law School? The day I walked into a room—I believe it was a small classroom—and found a tall very dark African man sitting in a chair? A man whose beauty was inseparable from his kindness, his devotion and caring, his big capable surgeon hands, his energy, his smile, his stillness and detachment. His eyes looking off into a distance, bloodshot, filled with nightmares and sorrow. *Handsome* was not the word. *Charismatic* would be the easy choice. But I see now the correct word would be *good*. As I sat onstage that night trying to interview him in front of five hundred people, I came face-to-face with a man who lived among the worst atrocities on the planet, who, as a gynecologist, had been forced day after day to heal and repair the bloodied, torn, eviscerated vaginas of a country that had been invaded, occupied, and pillaged for thirteen years. Or was it my first trip to Bukavu and meeting Christine, Mama C, the tall, stunning, outrageous warrior woman dressed in her brightly colored African finery and even taller in high heels who was my translator and guide through the journey with the survivors,

Mama C's bitter-heart-hurt-mama strength? Or was it
the women survivors who gathered for days outside
the room at Panzi Hospital to tell their stories? It was the
women, of course it was the women. Shaking women,
weeping women, women with missing limbs and repro-
ductive organs, women with machete lashes across their
faces and arms and legs, women limping on crutches,
women carrying babies the color of their rapists,
women who smelled like urine and feces because they
had fistulas—holes between their vaginas and bladder
and rectum—and now they were leaking, leaking.
Women who were funny, passionate, clever, and fierce,
who turned ten dollars into a thriving business. They
danced when they couldn't walk. They sang when their
futures had been stolen. Dr. Mukwege and Mama C,
the women and the Congo, let's not forget the Congo.
The silky, powder-blue Lake Kivu; the sweet, warm
African air that embraces; the high, green, fertile trees
and shocking orange and pink blossoms and birds; the
crazy, chattering morning birds. I was a goner for the
Congo.

Dr. Deb offered to bring her team from the Mayo
Clinic to support Dr. Mukwege at the Panzi Hospital
in Bukavu. I was the activist who would help her
make this happen. She had not been my doctor. I had

not been her patient. I had not been anyone's patient. I was an activist. I did not get sick.

I find myself dialing her number. She answers. I cannot breathe. I whisper. "They have found a tumor. It is very large. It has broken through, invaded the sides of my colon. They are not sure where it's coming from. It could be my uterus. Maybe you can help me."

She says, "Get on a plane. Come here. Come now."

SOMNOLENCE

There was something not only passive but downright suicidal about my response to the early signs of my cancer. A kind of resignation possessed me, as if I were an estranged voyeur noting my body from a great distance. *Somnolent* is the word that keeps coming to me. Half awake, half asleep, knowing but refusing to know. Somnolence: A self-produced narcotic state triggered by extreme danger, a kind of splintering of self, a partial leaving of one world with one foot or semiconsciousness in another. Somnolence: paralysis that comes when strung between two extreme moral choices—loyalty or shame, change or die. Many of my early years were lived in this semi-sleep. There I did not have to confront the twisted agony of betraying my mother each time my father found me in bed in the middle of the night. I did not have to try to unravel the madness of what it meant that the person I loved the most in the world was exploiting me, raping me, abusing me. I did not have to experience any conflict because none of it was really happening. We do this. Think climate change. All the early warning signs are here: heat waves, sea levels rising, flooding, glaciers melting, earlier springs, coral reefs bleeding, diseases spreading. All of it happening right in front of us. Just like the blood that first came from my vagina five years after I had stopped bleeding, my strange swollen belly, the terrible indigestion and the slightly sick feeling in my stomach. Then the blood in my poop and my wanting it to be hemorrhoids although I knew it wasn't hemorrhoids. Staring for minutes at the red swirl in the toilet, a clear marker that my end was near. I knew it of course. We all know everything. I said it to my close friends. Something was wrong. I knew when the size and shape of my poop suddenly changed and became skinny, something was wrong. It felt as if there was something blocking my insides. I knew it, but where did I go? Why didn't I fight for my body? Because in order to fight I would have had to face what was wrong. Because this couldn't be happening to me. Because secretly I didn't think my fighting would make a difference and I was going to die and I might as well die now. Because I was sick of suffering and pain and I wanted to die. Because I was madly attached to life and I simply could not bear the depth of my attachment.

The signs accumulated. But I did not respond. I would not wake up. We will not wake up. This terrifying sleep of denial. Is it an underlying belief that we as a human species are not worth it? Do we secretly feel we have lost our right to be here in all our selfishness and stupidity, our cruelty and greed?

All I know is that I waited too long. The tumor moved like an irrepressible army, like CO_2 through the atmosphere. It touched and destroyed and eroded and suddenly it was too late. I had not been a good steward to my body. I was afraid to ruffle feathers, afraid to make noise in the dark. Afraid to say what was happening. Then it would be real, then all fantasies would die. Then I would have to take responsibility. You are touching me where you should not be touching me. This is wrong. This is incest. Then I would be calling my father out. I would lose my father and the future and the love and safety and life itself. Then I would be outside the circle—alone. My old boyfriend used to say you have to choose between family and dignity. But I think the choice is deeper. I think it's a choice between being awake or half asleep. Being alert, not surrendering to the drowsiness, the delicious and comforting somnolence that will in the end be the death of us all.

CANCER TOWN

How to describe Rochester, Minnesota? It is essentially cancer town. There is one massive hospital complex called the Mayo Clinic, the thirty thousand people who work there, and everything else in the town exist either to support or supply it. Rochester is simultaneously something out of a bizarre sci-fi-we-destroyed-the-Earth future and the most ordinary middle-American town. It is kindness incarnate, almost frighteningly so. Everyone knows that everyone who comes there is finding out if they're sick, already sick, getting better from being sick, or too sick and will probably die. The whole town is like one palliative care unit. The waitresses are grief counselors. They serve you hamburgers and hold your hand as you weep for your son, daughter, mother, father, wife, or husband. All the sales people, the street cleaners, the airport shuttle drivers have an eye out for the wounded. There

are wig stores on every corner. In the one upscale restaurant you see people in wheelchairs hooked up to
their IVs having dinner or sitting outside stealing a
smoke on the street. In the Marriott Hotel every room
is filled with a sick person or a person hoping not to be
sick. If you have been in massive denial up to this point
about illness and how many people, for example, have
cancer, this would be the end of your denial. If you
were afraid to take in the inevitability of illness visiting
your body, this would be your "holy shit" moment. I
cannot say if cancer town was a comfort or a horror.
Like everything in America it was huge and consuming. I was wary. It reminded me of going to Disney
World and dropping acid. Things were going very
smoothly until I suddenly realized that we were inside
a totally perfect consumer bubble and that even the
horse's shit was being collected in little pans before it
hit the ground. All unpleasantness had been removed
so that the people could be happy, happy, happy. On
acid I began to panic that I would be forever stuck in
this happy land and that just entering it meant they had
laid siege to my mind. As I began to have the worst
bummer trip of my life I remember feeling grateful for
the anxiety because it defied this world of Pluto and
Donald Duck, this world of animated automated ampu-
tated America.

But I was not tripping now in Rochester. The diagnosis was so out of the blue, so shocking it had propelled me unwittingly into a kind of trance, and as I made my way through the homogenized, sanitized, Muzak-singing world I was grateful to be overwhelmed by beige.

DR. HANDSOME

The most handsome doctor in the world comes in to examine my rear end. What else, of course? I am obviously shell-shocked. I lie on the table, my underpants around my ankles, and think this is it. This is what the end feels like. The most handsome man in the world knowing that I have some horrible tumor inside my colon or rectum or uterus and that he has to feel it. I have already died from the humiliation and terror that are now merged in a cocktail of sweat and nausea, and I am curled on the table, hoping he will not see me, that I will disappear, and at the same time all I want is for him to see me and for this to be part of what it means to be human, and at that moment Dr. Handsome walks from one side of the examining table, where he is facing my back and naked ass, around to the other side, and he looks me in the eyes and says, "Before we begin, I want you to know how much I admire you and all you have done in this world for women and all you have written and all the ways you have made the world better. It is a privilege to care for you and I will do my very best." I feel like a little shaking dog picked up by a stranger in the rain, and this moment makes everything that follows in the next days bearable, and I know I can trust him with my body and I bet he will save my life. Doctors never believe how simple it is to give patients dignity. It takes a sentence. It takes a short walk around a table.

WHAT WE DON'T KNOW
GOING INTO SURGERY

Whether it's in my liver. How many nodes are involved. Whether I will need a bag—that is, an ileostomy bag. Whether the bag will be permanent. Whether they will be able to find it all or get it all.

They don't say: We don't know whether you will wake up, or have a bad response to all that cutting and bleeding and anesthesia. They don't say: We don't know if you will ever be the same, or what it will be like when the scar tissue forms and feels like rawhide under your skin, or how well you will handle the abscess that may follow the operation.

I try to imagine what it looks like inside without a uterus, cervix, ovaries. What will my vagina be connected to? I didn't know the difference between my rectum and my anus. Do you? I didn't know I was attached to my uterus. I never really thought about it.

They don't say: There will be this huge absence.

Or that we may have to take some of your vagina.

I am glad they didn't say that. Between the bag and the liver, there was enough to think about, and the idea of dying from cancer in my vagina was just too fucking ironic and weird.

I don't tell them they're removing what seems like a tumor but is really a flesh monument inside me. Huge and round. A taut ball of cellular yarn spun out of the stories of women, made of tears, silent screams, rocking torsos, and the particular loneliness of violence. A flesh creature birthed out of the secrets of brutality, each blood vessel a ribbon of story. My body has been sculpting this tumor for years, molding the pieces of pain, the clay residue of memories. It is a huge work and it has taken everything.

I do know that the night before the surgery, my dear friends gather in my room, and Kim—who is obsessed with ritual and has memorized about a thousand poems, which spill out of her in any emotional situation or moment like iambic Tourette's, insists that I state my intention with this whole journey and I think in my head, uh, surviving . . .

But I say, I do not want to be afraid.

I want to get rid of my fear, any fear, and then she flashes her deck of turquoise poem cards and says, "Pick one." And I pick:

THE JOURNEY
Mary Oliver

One day you finally knew
what you had to do, and began,
though the voices around you
kept shouting
their bad advice—
though the whole house
began to tremble
and you felt the old tug
at your ankles.
"Mend my life!"
each voice cried.
But you didn't stop.
You knew what you had to do,
though the wind pried
with its stiff fingers
at the very foundations—
though their melancholy
was terrible.
It was already late

enough, and a wild night,
and the road full of fallen
branches and stones.
But little by little,
as you left their voices behind,
the stars began to burn
through the sheets of clouds,
and there was a new voice,
which you slowly
recognized as your own,
that kept you company
as you strode deeper and deeper
into the world,
determined to do
the only thing you could do—
determined to save
the only life you could save.

I have been sober for almost thirty-three years and it is crazy how much I am looking forward to being drugged, I mean super drugged, out for the count, not dead but surely not here. Here is too much—the bag, something in my liver, a missing uterus, men wearing masks cutting into my body. The nodes. What the fuck is a node? Then there's my son who I adopted because his first mother died. My friends who look very worried. Getting up at 4:00 a.m. to be put to sleep. An enema first thing. My mother who is not here. My mother who I haven't told because I don't want to worry her. The women of the Congo who don't have the luxury of drugs or CAT scans or bags.

Saving my own life.

THIS IS WHERE YOU WILL
CROSS THE UJI RIVER

It's dark in cancer town when we get up. Toast, Kim, and Paula walk me from the hotel to the hospital. We are all dazed from Valium. They are holding me by my arms, propping me up, and no one is saying a word. I feel like Gary Gilmore on his way to being executed at Utah State Prison. I believe he was killed by a firing squad, four shots to his heart. This could easily be my last morning, and there isn't even any bloody sun. My final memory will be the last thing resembling beauty, the faux Pakistani carpets in the Marriott Hotel lobby. It's dark in Tumor Town, but it's prime time, busy. There are so many of us online at 4:30 a.m. that it feels like the airport. The crowd is midwestern and over-weight, starving and empty from last night's enemas and cleansers. The Mayo workers are way too cheerful for this time of day. But here in the Cancer Airways

terminal there is no time. There are just the sick and
the people who help the sick, the people who are about
to be put to sleep and the ones who will put them to
sleep. There are the madly chipper airline workers and
the rest of us who are all going somewhere with our
matching plastic heart-you ID bracelets but who are
not so sure if and how we're coming back.

I relinquish my clothes and my jewelry and attempt to
wrap myself in the skimpy hospital gown. I find some
comfort in the bare cotton blankets. After endless
bathroom trips from the final enema, and after I have
tried not to worry my friends by being too dramatic
and saying things like, "If I don't come back, please
give my books to . . . ," they come to wheel me away.
As I climb onto the gurney, I understand why you don't
walk into the operating room. Your bare legs just
wouldn't take you there. There is no one going with
me on this trip. This one's on my own. This one is the
big one.

I see Toast and Kim and Paula waving. I flash them
the V and give them the best smile I can and I close my
eyes. I am standing in the wide-open field in Panzi at
City of Joy in Bukavu. It is right after one of those mad
Congo downpours. The Earth is wet and green and
now the sun is just breaking out. The mountains are in

the distance. I see the buildings are finished. I see the women strong and moving from class to class. They are becoming leaders and revolutionaries. I see them cooking and dancing. Mama C and Dr. Mukwege are greeting me. Alisa is there and Jeanne and Alfonsine and Mama Bachu. I have made a promise. That is all that matters. Keeping my promise. I do not think about all the people who are suddenly standing around the gurney in masks and gowns with needles and machines and tape. I do not think about what they will find inside me, that I could wake up with a death sentence or never wake up. I do not think that my mother is not there and my father is dead. I do not even notice how much I am shivering from the freezing cold. I am in Bukavu. It is hot there. I am in the sun. I keep my promises.

You must be firmly resolved. Do not begrudge your fief; do not think of your wife and children. And do not depend on others. You must simply make up your mind. The reason that you have survived until now when so many have died was so that you would meet with this affair. This is where you will cross the Uji River. This is where you will ford the Seta. This will determine whether you win honor or disgrace your name. This is what is meant when it is said that it is difficult to be born as a human being, and that it is

difficult to believe in the Lotus Sutra. You should
pray intently that Shakyamuni, Many Treasures and
the Buddhas of the ten directions will all gather and
enter into your body to assist you.

The Writings of Nichiren Daishonin, Volume 1

TWO QUESTIONS

I open my eyes as they are wheeling me down a long corridor and my sister suddenly comes into focus. She is standing next to Dr. Deb. I am sure I have died. I have not spoken to my sister in years. They are both smiling at me. Well, my sister is trying to smile. There is something about her trying that makes me want to cry. My face is not yet attached to me, so I do not know how to cry or smile. I hear myself saying through strange things that appear to be my lips, "Is it in my liver?" Dr. Deb says, "No." "Do I have a bag?" Dr. Deb says, "Yes, but it's temporary." Okay. It is not in my liver. My bag is temporary. My sister is here. Blackout.

UTERUS = HYSTERIA

There are bags and tubes coming out of every orifice of a body I soon realize is my own. I can do nothing but push my oxycodone magic button. This is a drug addict's dream. Only the hint of pain, the thought of pain, the "could be" pain, and I hit my button. The nurses, with their Rochester, Minnesota, accent, ask me, "What is your pain, Eve? Can you tell me, from one to ten?" In the beginning I just say 8. It feels like a good number and everyone will feel fine with me hitting the button. I am sure it is an exaggeration. But I don't know. Maybe my pain is 8. It all depends on 10. Is 10 wailing, scream-ing out, bent-over near-dead pain? Then 8 must be close to that. It isn't really 8 then, but the tubes and the bags account for something, if only just being totally freaked out. Maybe I am 6. The oxycodone keeps me floating, so really there is very little pain. Maybe the memory of the pain is now stored away, like winter clothes, together with the memory of the surgery that was wiped out by the amnesia drugs and, they say, will never come back. It would be awfully scary to be at some fancy dinner party or having sex when suddenly the vivid consuming flash of your stomach being sliced wide open like a fish or pig returns. Did I tell you they cut right through my belly button? Did I tell you I was always afraid of my belly button, afraid even to touch it? It gave me the serious creeps. When I would wash it or clean it with Q-tips, I would always have to hold my breath. Slicing through my umbilicus, the only evidence I was once connected to my mother, the place where her blood and my blood were one. And did I tell you she got very sick right after they cut through my belly button? Right after they removed my uterus, my ovaries, my cervix, fallopian tubes, lymph nodes, lymph channels, the top part of my vagina, and the tissue in the pelvic cavity that surrounds the cervix and all my mother parts. No, that comes later.

What is most pressing now is, Why cancer in my uterus? Uterus: a hollow muscular organ in the pelvic cavity of female mammals, in which the embryo is nourished and develops before birth.

I try to imagine my uterus accommodating this tumor the way it might have once held a baby. I almost had two of them. Babies. Is there a point to a uterus if you do not make a baby? Was the tumor a way of growing something? Was I growing a trauma baby?

I remember years ago—when I was going through a period when I seemed to be sick all the time—a shrink friend saying to me in that knowing and slightly patronizing sorry-for-me way, "You somatize, Eve." *Somatize*. It was one of those words like individuate. I had to look it up. *Somatize*: how the body defends itself against too much stress, manifesting psychological distress as physical symptoms in the stomach or nerves or uterus or vagina. I read that women who had suffered physical, emotional, and sexual abuse tended to somatize more.

It turns out that somatization is related to hysteria, which stems from the Greek cognate of uterus, ὑστέρα (hysteria). Uterus = hysteria. They always called me hysterical in my family. Extreme feeling. Sarah Bernhardt. Intense. But what is extreme? Again, it depends on 10? I mean, what would be the appropriate level of emotional response to someone beating you daily or calling you jackass or stupid or molesting you. What would be the nonhysterical response to living in a world where so many are eating dirt and swimming in the sewage system in Port-au-Prince to unclog the drains and find plastic bottles to sell? What would be the appropriate nonhysterical response to people blindfolding other people and walking them around naked on leashes or watching waving people being abandoned on rooftops in a flood? What would be the proper way to experience these things? *Hysteria*—a word to make women feel insane for knowing what they know. A word that has so many implications—hysterical, out of control, insane, can't take her seriously, raving. Hysteria is caused by suffering from a huge trauma where there is an underlying conflict. What was my conflict? Loving my mother and father, betraying my mother when my father molested me, wanting my father all to myself even if it hurt my mother? Witnessing and hearing the most horrific stories in the world inflicted on women's bodies and being unable to stop it in spite of every effort? Wanting to fall in love and being totally unable to trust, hungering for connection and always finding it claustrophobic. What doesn't cause or produce conflicted feelings? What isn't traumatizing?

So, does removing my uterus mean they have removed my hysteria? I don't feel any less hysterical. Actually, the tubes and bags and needles are making me feel quite upset and I wonder if there is such a thing as rape cancer. Do I have rape cancer? Do we get it if we have been molested or traumatized or raped? Are there rape cancer cells that get formed at the moment of violation and then get released into the bloodstream at another moment of trauma later in life? How many women with vaginal and uterine and ovarian cancer have been raped or beaten or traumatized? Does anyone know? Would Mayo do a study? Is there a way to cure rape cancer? Does each future trauma release more rape cancer cells? Is trauma cancer? Is this kind of obsessing the reason I am sick?

Am I hysterical? Alert! 8 8 8, maybe even 9. I hit the oxycodone button.

FALLING, OR CONGO STIGMATA

There are no accidents. Or maybe everything is an accident. My friend Paul says to me, "It's like you've got Congo Stigmata." Well, actually, almost everyone said it in one way or another. "It doesn't surprise me, Eve, of course. All those stories of rape over all these years. The women have entered you." And at first I pushed this away because it's not really a great advertisement for activism. Come care about others, listen to their stories and their pain, and you can contract it too. Then immediately after the surgery, the doctors told me that they had discovered something inside me that they had rarely seen before. Cells of endometrial (uterine) cancer had created a tumor between the vagina and the bowel and had "fistulated" the rectum. Essentially, the cancer had done exactly what rape had done to so many thousands of women in the Congo. I ended up having the same surgery as many of them.

Dr. Handsome, my colon doctor, e-mailed Dr. Deb the day after the surgery and said he had been unable to sleep because he was so in awe of the mystery of what they had found. He said, "These findings are not medical, they are not science. They are spiritual."

I have always been drawn to holes. Black holes. Infinite holes. Impossible holes. Absences. Gaps, tears in membranes. Fistulas. Obstetric fistulas occur because of extended difficult labor. Necessary blood is unable to flow to the tissues of the vagina and the bladder. As a result, the tissues die and a hole forms through which urine or feces flow uncontrollably. In the Congo fistulas have been caused by rape, in particular gang rape, and rape with foreign objects like bottles or sticks. So many thousands of women in eastern Congo have suffered fistulas from rape that the injury is considered a crime of combat.

After three trips to the Congo, I needed to see a fistula. I asked to sit in on a reparative operation. I needed to know the shape of this hole, the size of this hole. I needed to know what a woman's insides looked like when her most essential cellular tissue had been punctured by a stick or a penis or penises. Wearing a mask and gown, I peered into this woman's vagina, as she lay on her back, legs spread, her feet tied to steel stirrups with strips of blue-green rags made from old hospital uniforms. As always, I was awed by the vagina, so intricate, so simple, so delicate. There in the lining was an undeniable hole, a rip, a tear in the essential story. It was almost a perfect circle, the size of a quarter maybe, too big to prevent things from getting in or from falling out. I couldn't help but think of the sky, of the membrane of the sky and the rip in the ozone. Humans had become hole makers. Bullet holes and drilled holes, hurt holes, greed holes, rape holes. Holes in membranes that function to protect the surface or bodily organ. Holes in the ozone layer that prevent the sun's ultraviolet light from reaching the Earth's surface. Holes that cause mutation of bacteria and viruses and an increase in skin cancers. Holes, gaps in our memory from trauma. Holes that destroy the integrity, the possibility of wholeness, of fullness. A hole that would determine the rest of this woman's life, would prevent her from holding her pee or poop, would destroy sex or make it very difficult, would undermine her having a baby, would require many painful operations and still might not be fixed. As I stood there in mask and gown, I realized I had stopped breathing. This woman's vagina was a map of the future, and I could feel myself falling, falling through the hole in the world, the hole in myself, the hole that was made when my father invaded me and I lost my way. The hole that was made when the social membrane was torn by incest. Falling through the hole in this woman, I was falling. I have always been falling. But this time was different.

LU

I open my eyes and my sister, Lu, is sitting by my bed. It is not a postsurgical hallucination. She is here. I close my eyes. I need time to take in her presence. I am not sure how I feel.

She is watching over me as if it were the most natural thing, as if we had never stopped talking and had been seeing each other regularly for years. She has simply resumed her place. I peek again.

It is Lu. I love my sister's face. Her skin is so soft. She has the hugest breasts, which I used to touch and it would make her crazy. They were bowls of comfort. My sister is comfort. Except when she is not. She is by my bed. I am suspicious. Is it pity? I hate pity. Is she finally in control? She is up. I am down. Is it guilt? My illness, proximity to death, unfinished business? Does she want to be here? Is it compulsion? Duty? Could it be care? I want it to be care. I don't know my sister. She just came. She just flew here. I like that. I am not sure. She is bossy. She will take charge. I like that.

I reach out and gently touch her hand. She is startled. We are both startled, but she takes my hand. We are both tentative. She smiles. I smile. My sister.

HERE'S WHAT'S GONE

Nine hours.

Rectum

sections of colon

uterus

ovaries

cervix

fallopian tubes

part of my vagina

seventy nodes

Here's what's new:

A rebuilt rectum made out of my colon

A stoma

A temporary ileostomy bag

A catheter in my bladder

My face, the size of two faces

A button I push

any time I begin to feel what

is missing.

THE STOMA

I don't remember, but they say the first thing I did when I woke up was ask to touch it. I can't imagine being that brave or wanting to be that brave, but there were a lot of drugs involved. And I have a history of needing to know and see things. It's not really bravery at all but more like terror of what's happening in the dark: the grown man's scented hand invading my six-year-old body, the selling of the Congolese mines in the back rooms of Kigali, the whispering posse of teenage girls organizing my public demise. It's why I became a chronic eavesdropper and an unashamed journal invader. I had to know. It gave me mastery. I pulled the curtains back. I opened the door. I controlled the entry of pain. So it doesn't surprise me that I needed to touch the red fleshy nipple made from my colon that was now magically outside my body. The stoma, a minimouth of sorts that was now directing my poop into the ileostomy bag. I was rubbing it and feeling it, like some gooey species you find in a cave, and I could tell it was grossing my sister out. She never liked to touch it or see it. We were opposites. When it was terrible in our house, and it was often terrible, she would suddenly not be there. She could disappear even if she was still in the room. It never occurred to me until after the cancer that I wasn't the brave one but the masochistic one. I mistook pain and hardship for a form of protection. My sister was afraid, so she acted afraid. I had never been brave enough to allow myself to be afraid. I had to outdo my father and beat him at his own game. Your hands choking my throat, your fist punching and bloodying my nose: These are nothing compared to what I can do to myself or what I can and will bring on myself.

Or maybe that wasn't it at all. Maybe the terror was familiar—the adrenaline buzz, the body-clutching, almost-dying sensation as my head bounced off the wall. Maybe that familiarity is what I came to associate with connection, aliveness, love, and why I was always drawn to violent men: men who didn't beat me, but who lived on the broken edge of explosion. Those men who could go there if pushed and I knew how to push because I needed to get a glimpse of that sugar love, needed to feel that snap zap hit of IhatehityouIhitneedyou. That's how the milk originally came to me— in smacks—in loud white yelping gulps.

I was touching my stoma and my sister was asking me why I needed to do that. I could tell the stoma freaked her out. She didn't want to feel it. It was like the accident on our fancy suburban road when we were kids. There was a lot of glass and blood, and we heard that a woman had gone through the windshield and had lost her ear. There was a group of men looking for her ear. I wanted to go and help them. I wanted to know what it would be like to stumble on an ear in the middle of our road. I wanted to be the one who said, "Here, here, I found her ear. There is time. It is still alive. She can get it put back on." My sister would not go with me. She would not be my copilot in the flight toward hardship and danger. She steered clear of it and me for many years. And why wouldn't she?

I drank myself mad, numbed myself with drugs at sixteen, snuck out with grown men to the Fillmore East for the late show, lived naked on communes, and stole things. I wrote my thesis on suicide in contemporary American poetry as I bartended and got laid on the pool table in the back. I was a caretaker in a Chelsea house for schizophrenics and a group leader in a homeless shelter on Thirtieth Street. I followed Joan of Arc's route around France and took the train to Rome at midnight and wore spiky high heels for an Italian leather dyke. I took acid for three days on the train from

Montreal to Vancouver where I had a one-night stand with a famous Muslim jazz player who seduced me with his saxophone and prayerful calling. I found my way into rape refugee camps in Bosnia, wore a burqa into the Taliban's Afghanistan, drove espresso-pumped through land-mined roads in Kosovo. I had to see it, know it, touch it, find the ear. Maybe I was playing out my badness, or searching for my goodness, or getting closer and closer to the deepest inhumanity to try to understand how to survive the very worst we are capable of. Then I went to the Congo and it was there that it all shattered. There where in one breath the most grotesque acts of evil were countered with the deepest kindness. I had gone there.

My stoma—my shit on the outside. There was no way to get used to that. So better outdo it, better touch the stoma, know the stoma, see the stoma and, despite my sister's protestations, I continued and I don't know why this little fleshy nipple made me feel suddenly maternal (it was most likely the drugs), made me want to caress my own body and protect her and myself for perhaps the first time in my life. Why it made me laugh a crazy, giddy laugh, as if the stoma nipple were a kind of baby born out of my flesh. I wanted to know it/her. My stoma was born and the birth announcement was

The End of My Invincibility. I could no longer hide my fleshy, exposed human parts.

With the help of a fabulous tough-love nurse, I learned to take care of my stoma—to clean her and put cream on her, wrap her properly, keep her from getting chafed or irritated; and I see now how this exposure, this shit-filled nipple of my vulnerability, was the pathway to mercy.

HOW'D I GET IT?

Was it tofu?

Was it failing at marriage twice?

Was it never having babies?

Was it having an abortion and a miscarriage?

Was it talking too much about vaginas?

Was it worry every day for fifty-seven years that I wasn't good enough?

Was it the pressure to fill Madison Square Garden with eighteen thousand or the Superdome with forty thousand?

Was it the exhaustion of trying to change?

Was it the city?

Was it the line of two hundred women repeated in hundreds of small towns for many years after each performance, after each speech, women lined up to show me their scars, wounds, warrior tattoos?

Was it suburban lawn pesticides?

Was it Chernobyl?

Three Mile Island?

Was it my father smoking Lucky Strikes and my mother smoking Marlboros?

Was it my father dying slowly and never calling to say good-bye?

Was it witnessing him insulting waiters in restaurants and me going back to give them my allowance?

Was it my mother's thinness and frailty?

Was it bad reviews?

Or good reviews?

Was it being reviewed?

Was it sleeping with men who were married?

Was it always being third?

Was it my first husband sleeping with my close friend?

Was it shopping and needing to shop?

Was it being a vegetarian for thirty years?

Was it Froot Loops?

Massive chlorine in swimming pools?

Was it Tab? I drank a lot of Tab after I got sober.

Was it Lilt (the toxic-smelling substance my mother used to perm my hair)?

Was it Tame (the solution she used to get the tangles out)?

Was it crinoline (the abusive and starchy material I was forced to wear underneath my dresses)?

Was it Shirley Temples? Ginger ale with red dye number two juice and a red dye number two cherry on top—a favorite for the sophisticated country-club alcoholic father.

Was it drinking water out of plastic bottles?

Not being breast-fed?

Canned chop suey?

TV dinners?

Was it turquoise Popsicles?

Was it Epstein-Barr?

Was it in my blood?

Was it already decided?

Was it deet?

Was it that I didn't cry enough?

Or cried too much?

Was it promiscuous sex?

All those arrests at nuclear power plants?

Sleeping in radioactive dust?

Was it my IUD?

Was it birth control pills?

Was it not enough boundaries?

Was it too many walls?

CIRCUMAMBULATING

There is a miniblackboard in my room and a red felt-tip pen, and each walk I take I get a check. I need six checks a day. The first days I only make two or three walks (one to the door of my room, which is about four steps and then back). I put down five red checks, which is a lie. I cannot believe I'm cheating, but no one is really buying it. Everything about the hospital is pushing me before I feel ready. I do not want to be awake. I do not want to learn how to change my bag. I definitely do not want to walk. There is a walker and I lean on it and I step, crawl, step, crawl clockwise in a circle around the nurse's stations outside my door. I am circumambulating around the nurses, who are without a doubt the object of my worship. Circumambulating like the Buddhists I once joined at the Jokhang Temple in Lhasa. They circle for hours in an attempt to reorient their minds in the direction of greater and more spontaneous compassion. The nurses here at Mayo—Monica, Rhonda, and Sarah—are my lamas. The tenderness and precision in the way they change me and turn the corners of my sheets, their kind but firm approach. The way they get delicious flavors into my ice chips.

Today my son makes the circuit with me. I feel old and ugly. My hair is limp since the surgery, and my skin is so pasty. I feel like a mangy dog I once saw in front of a temple in Kathmandu. He clearly had rabies and was foaming at the mouth. A monk told me that all the hungry, scuzzy dogs who hung around the temples were really lamas and priests who had never reached enlightenment. I had a photograph of that scabby dog above my desk for years as a reminder to work on my shit. Now I was "mangy dog with son." He didn't push me and this worried me. For years he had been my sadistic workout coach, punishing me beyond all limits. My son who I adopted when he was fifteen and I was twenty-three. I was married to his father. I wanted to protect him. I always did. My son's mother, Diane, and I looked a lot alike. When she got shot my son was five, and he saw them wheel out her bloody body. They never told him she had died. He waited for a year and she didn't come back. So I work super hard to never leave.

Now he was very quiet beside me. I could hear the inner workings of his brain—each step in the circumambulation a recalculation and an assimilation of my proximity to death. I wanted to take his hand and say, "Listen, buddy, I am not going to die, okay? I am not your bad karma or your endless merciless abandonment story. I will never leave you, remember? I made a deal." But something in me couldn't say it. Maybe this was the moment where it changed. We're old now. I'm fifty-six. You're two years away from fifty. Maybe right now I don't have answers. Not for you, my son. Not for anyone. Maybe the high tide grabbed our canoe when we weren't looking and we're suddenly out at sea. Maybe all we do now is row and move with the currents and hold on to each other when it gets rough and be happy if and when and where we land. Maybe I have no more offerings, only this emptiness that I am willing to share.

ICE CHIPS

I had a bisected colon, a missing rectum, a bag, and absolutely no idea how food was even going to work or where it would end up. In my visual imagination, all my missing organs and remaining organs were confused. And yet all I could think about was a hamburger. When the pain got bad or I started hallucinating free-floating cancer cells, I meditated on hamburgers—the meat and the bun. I could taste the blood. I wanted the blood and the grilled hamburger juice. I wanted the condiments, the tomato and lettuce and pickles and ketchup. I wanted to hold the hamburger in my hands. I wanted to be a normal, healthy person sitting in my bed eating a hamburger. Was it nostalgia for those rare moments before I turned sixteen and swore off meat, when we were allowed to have hamburgers and we ate in the kitchen, which meant my father wasn't there (he never ate with the children or the help in the kitchen), and there might be fun, a moment of fun? So maybe hamburgers meant fun. Maybe the nostalgia was for what wasn't—a normal, happy hamburger family with French fries on the side on a Saturday night. Maybe the hamburger was comfort. Or maybe it was defiance. I had been a rather righteous vegetarian for twenty years and I had come out of the surgery wanting meat. I was going to eat meat, I was going to stop being so good, so perfect, so hummus-tofu-lite.

Meat had always repulsed me. But now I was out for blood. I could have had fangs. I shocked myself and my friends, Pat and Carole. They said they thought it might be too much to go from a thimbleful of Jell-O to a hamburger. I said I felt a hamburger was my ticket back. They seemed disturbed, as if I was a lifelong Communist suddenly selling hedge funds. They needed me to be who I had always been for them. I said a lot of things had changed. I had cancer, for example, and lost organs and had a bag. They wanted me to be happy. That is all they wanted, and they wanted me to stay alive. They went shopping in Rochester and came back with wildly colored pajamas and socks. They arranged my flowers and adjusted my pillows. They sat with me through several of my hardest nights and ended up sleeping in my room on crazy cardboard cots. They made me laugh and bonded with the nurses, and eventually they got me the hamburger. They did. They even served it on a plate with fries. I don't know if I am inventing this, but I believe there was a group of loved ones, a stunned audience around the bed, as I ate it. Even the senior nurse, Monica, pulled up a chair. I didn't mind them watching. I needed witnesses. Something was coming from my body, this call for flesh and blood. I was eating, devouring. I could not stop it. It felt obscene almost, transgressive to be this open, this naked, this hungry.

It reminded me of visiting the lions in the park at the Mara in Masailand, Kenya. About thirty cars were gathered around one spot. Families and couples from all over the world were frozen watching a huge lion dragging the carcass of a zebra across a field. It turns out lions don't even chew. They just bite with their massive jaws and swallow. The lion had no shame, but she had no pride either. Something inside her was compelling her to do what she needed to do and she was doing it. It was that simple: survival. No need for apologies, no need for applause.

I watched that lion with the same horror and delight that I saw on the faces of my friends around my hospital bed. I ate way too fast. I ate every bite. Later that evening, my body shut down like a lawn mower with a big stick jammed in the gears. They called it an obstruction and I vomited . . . a lot. I was on ice chips for the next ten days and lost almost twenty pounds, but I was lion.

PATIENT

"You have done many things," said this very beautiful, very tiny Italian doctor who appeared one day in my room like a gnome. "But you have never been a patient. Now you will learn to be a patient. This will be hard for you." He was cryptic and correct. The last thing I wanted to be was a patient. I didn't like sick people. First of all, they were sick. Sick was not well, not able, not working, not making things better. Sick was surrendering, caving in. Sick was wasting time, not adding up. Sick was alone and stuck as the rest of the well world moved by.

For some bizarre reason I am wearing sunglasses in my hospital bed. (I look swollen and horrible and because of all the drugs I think a little lipstick, sunglasses, and my pink knit cap make me look better, but in fact I look insane.) I am wearing sunglasses hoping the gnome man cannot see my eyes or hear my thoughts, which are spinning out of control at the mere suggestion of being a patient. There is obviously something scaring me even more than the cancer. It is the idea of stopping. The idea of being still. Of not being able to do or make or travel, or speak or organize or write. I don't want to be a fucking patient. Then the Italian doctor says, "It will be a threshold for you. You will learn to have pity for yourself. You will learn to be a patient." In that moment I want to wrap my IV tube around his neck and jerk it hard.

As part of me rages and refuses, another part of me is already there. I watch it there and it knows, truly knows, something else. This part of me likes the gnome, wants to crawl up on his lap and be his patient. This part is so tired. This part knows he is telling the truth, he is a guide, giving me a challenge, a vision, saying, "This is it. Your life has to change. It cannot be driven anymore by a need to prove anything. It cannot be a reaction, a 'fuck you,' an 'I'll show you.' That's how you got sick. That is what your sickness is: overtaxing the body, the nervous system, fight-or-flight, always driving off the imagined enemy, always pushing and driving yourself, pushing and fighting and driving." I am too tired now. I have cancer. My organs are gone. I have tubes coming out of me, and a bag. My body is sewn up the center. There is no drive. I can't find the gears. I am a patient. Patient. Patient. And something relaxes in the center of me for the first time since I heard my father raise his voice, and I sleep, I really sleep.

THE RUPTURE/THE GULF SPILL

At Sloan-Kettering they show it to me on the CAT scan screen: a huge pool of blackness in the center of me— the same day as the Gulf oil spill, the now poisoned Gulf of Mexico somehow inside me. Sixteen ounces of pus. Two point five two million gallons of oil a day. An intra-abdominal abscess. Contamination from postsurgery, postexplosion leaking, the spread of infection to the bloodstream to the ocean. My body is rupturing, shit leaking from where they closed it up, leaking there and spilling, purging—same moment, same day BP exploding rising up, gushing out of me from every orifice, nothing can stop it, trying to shut it down, but not able, there is no stopping it, and it smells putrid, otherworldly, and it fills the bag and I can't get to the bathroom and the bag explodes and I am puking, my guts still sewn raw from the surgery, and it really hurts.

Symptoms may include abdominal pain, chills,

diarrhea, oil penetration destroying the plumage of birds, making them less able to float in the water, less able to escape when being attacked, preening leads to kidney damage, altered liver function, ruptured digestive tracts, lack of appetite, nausea, dolphins spurting oil through their blow holes, rectal tenderness and fullness, seal fur reduced in its insulation abilities, leading to hypothermia, vomiting, weakness.

They need to start the chemotherapy, but they can't until the infection is gone. I'm too weak and there will be too many complications. Chemo compromises your immune system and I am a sea of infection. They will need to suck it out of me. Treatment of an intra-abdominal abscess requires antibiotics (given intravenously) and drainage. Drainage involves placing a needle through the skin into the abscess, usually under X-ray guidance. The drain is then left in place for days or weeks, until the abscess goes away.

After two false starts, BP engineers successfully insert a mile-long tube into the broken riser pipe to divert some of the oil to a drill ship on the surface. Over nine days, the tube siphons off about twenty-two thousand barrels of oil, which is just a fraction of the total spill.

Over the next three weeks, the Sloan-Kettering team will insert tubes on three different occasions into the center of my abscess to drain the pus. The first time I am wheeled into the operating room, I decide to wear sunglasses because it is so bright and I feel too exposed. There is a madly arrogant rock-and-roll surgeon dude who treats my body like some beat-up practice guitar. He tells me to keep my sunglasses on because they're hot (and he doesn't mean me). Then, before I know it, he is driving a thick needle attached to a catheter tube through my surgical wound and I yell and tell him it really hurts, but he doesn't stop or drug me properly or even seem to hear me. I scream more and he just keeps going. I hate his guts. I am crying and I feel like some groupie chick who's decided too late that she doesn't want to have sex with the band in the back of the van, but no one is listening.

Afterward I meet with my oncology team, who seem utterly distracted. I explain that this procedure really hurt and I'm super weak from the infection and have lost a lot of weight. They tell me they can only begin chemo when the infection is gone and that they have been waiting for me. I feel as if I have failed and that my cancer cells are psychotically subdividing as we speak. They want me to consider radiation. They send me to another distracted, testy, arrogant doctor dude who makes me feel that my questions are childish and wasting his time. He tells me that they were planning to radiate the place where my cancer was but that scar tissue has already formed around my intestines and they don't dance and move the way they should (again my fault). There is a risk that the radiation could zap the same intestine section over and over, and if that happens I would probably never be able to eat again and I would have a permanent bag. And so I ask my irritating questions: Is the radiation necessary? "We don't know." Is radiation more effective than chemo? "We don't think so." Are radiation and chemo more effective together? "We are not sure." Is chemo more effective than radiation for uterine cancer? "Yes, we know it is."

Then why, I ask, are you even thinking of radiation if it could destroy my intestines and make it impossible for me to eat or poop again? He says, "It's up to you. Only you can decide. We have given you the data." Implicit in this is my impending wrong decision. And I say, "What would you do if this were your body?" trying to bring his body into the room. And he says, "Can't say." And I say again, annoying him further, "But if you do not know if it will help, why are you putting me in the position where I have to choose?" Then he says the mantra of the end of the world. "WE LIKE TO THROW EVERYTHING AT IT. That's all we know how to do." And I say, "The only problem is that IT is attached to ME." And I swear, he doesn't flinch. Me is irrelevant. Me is personal and specific. Me is what has to be passed through to get to where he is going. Me is what can be sacrificed to get better information. And I suddenly know what the bride in Pakistan felt when the drones bombed her wedding and her fiancé splintered into pieces and her mother was only fragments of dress. They were throwing everything at al-Qaeda. And I suddenly love my infection and my protective scar tissue, which are saving me from the everything they want to throw at me.

Later Dr. Deb tells me that she worked with a genius brain surgeon and mentor who performed operations trying to remove cancerous brain tumors, and most of the time his patients died. She once asked him why he chose to go into that field when he had so few successes, and he said, "Because sometimes I do have a success, and that is worth all the failures." He was able to begin to trace what the successes had in common—all the patients had abscess infections in their wounds after surgery, and he believed that in fighting off the infections, their bodies ended up fighting off the cancer as well, that in fact abscess infections could be curative.

Maybe I was reaching for straws. But I like straws. I return home and I embrace my abscess. It is kicking my ass, but it is kicking my immune fighting system into gear. I need my abscess. I put on my signed Muhammad Ali gloves. I box with myself in the mirror. I watch *When We Were Kings* for the sixth time. Kinshasa. Ali and Foreman. The Rumble in the Jungle. Biggest upset in history. That's what I'm going for. It was Ali's staying power. Foreman was young. He gave him everything he had in the first rounds, just like this infection. Ali stayed on the ropes absorbing the hundreds of blows to his body. Even Ali's greatest supporters had their money on Foreman. But he was fighting for other things, bigger things. He dropped Foreman in the eighth round.

BECOMING SOMEONE ELSE

I call Mama C every single day. It doesn't matter if I am drugged after surgery or in terrible pain or depressed. I sit up straight. I change my voice. I become someone else. Mama C, besieged by corrupt contractors and dysfunctional UNICEF management, by cement that can't be transported on roads that don't exist, by prices that escalate by the hour, by the lack of water or electricity, by massacres in encroaching villages, by downpours that are so heavy and intense that untended babies get washed away. I call Mama C every single day. People tell me I am too sick for these calls. But honestly, I live for them. For fifteen or thirty minutes, sometimes an hour, I push past my own darkness and terror, past my weakness and nausea, and travel. I get to hear stories. I ask Christine to describe the morning. She tells me about the startling, diverse chorus of birds and how she didn't sleep due to the singing that went on all night and all week from the neighbors' funeral. She describes eating the perfect mango and the just-ripe avocados from her tree, and how Justine and her troupe performed *The Vagina Monologues*, causing disruptions and discussions about vaginas and rape in the village churches. She tells me how there were suddenly cows on Essence Road, which held up traffic for three hours. She tells me how no one will be allowed to take pictures of women survivors at City of Joy when it opens because it is not a zoo. She tells me about Dr. Mukwege's dear friend whose children were macheted on the road, how the wife was stabbed and lost her mind, and no one has any idea who did it or why.

She tells me that we will grow a huge vegetable garden, and I ask if we can have goats. We talk about staff and training and funding and opening, and we dream of the revolution that will come after the first thousand women graduate and return home to their communities. Sometimes Mama C is very depressed and I use my strength to cheer her. Sometimes she lies to me and pretends everything is better than it is. It is almost impossible for me to complain. Cancer is rarely talked about in the Congo. The word is hardly used. When people get it, it is usually too late because there is no CAT scan machine in all of Bukavu and the Kivus. The women who have fistulas are incontinent and they will leak for life because they are not lucky enough to be given bags. Some are even sent into solitary exile in the forests. Jeanne has had eight operations. Alfonsine is held together with tubes and prayers. Yet both of them spend their lives taking care of other women.

Mama C is Belgian and Congolese. She calls me Ev and worries about Ev in the chemio. Chemio. It sounds like a board game or maybe even something lucky. We do not talk about her fear that I will die and leave her alone with City of Joy. We do not talk about Dr. Muk-wege, who is devastated by my cancer.

Several years ago we organized a huge march and demonstration. At least five thousand women took to the streets of Bukavu to protest the rapes, the war, and the torture. We ended up in a huge field. The interna-tional community, the elites, and the First Lady sat under a canopy while the thousands of poor women who had been violated and abandoned stood in the unforgiving sun. There was no platform to give a speech, just a wooden carton. I looked like a not-so-cool white female Che Guevara. I had been marching all day and was wearing a black cap. The First Lady looked like Princess Di on acid, in shocking pink with a hat the size of the Kinshasa. Christine was translating for me. But something miraculous happened as we stood on the wobbly carton, our arms around each other's waists in order not to fall. She was exceedingly tall and I looked very tiny. There was one microphone. I must have begun the speech, but honestly I don't know which one of us gave it. She finished my English sentences in French. Our bodies were no longer separate. We were one unit of female resistance exploding on a box in a field in the Congo.

BEWARE OF GETTING THE BEST

I am a pool of pus oil on a couch. I have two bags now: One drains the abscess, the other, poop. The infection and the antibiotics and Xanax have made me weak and I have lost my appetite. I find myself staring endlessly at the video of oil gushing into the gulf. There are oil-drenched pelicans and dead baby dolphins washing up, and it turns out I don't need a uterus to be hysterical. All my caretakers, particularly Lu, are furious and try to turn the video off, but it is bizarrely comforting to watch the spill. I really don't mind dying. I mean, who wants to live in a world where the ocean is bleeding? Did I tell you that my mother lives on the Gulf of Mexico and that it is her favorite place? Did I tell you one thing I love about my mother is how she can identify every egret, seagull, and pelican? She has given them names. My mother knows when the dolphins arrive—the season and the time of day. Even if she is in her apartment, she can feel they are out there. Sometimes she just stops what's she doing and runs out to the porch as if they've called her. I know that oil on her beach would kill my mother, who is already so thin and frail from three different bouts of cancer in the last thirty years; one was in her thyroid, one took her lung, and the last and most recent one was in her bladder. I am in the third hour of video-cam oil-spill gazing when Lu comes in and takes my computer away from me. I am sure she is going to lecture me, but she gently and tentatively says, "It's back." "What?" I say. "The cancer, Mom's cancer is back . . . in her bladder. We weren't going to tell you, but it's serious. She will have to have an operation." I don't look at Lu. I turn back to the oil spill.

Later that evening my bag explodes again and the horrible smell returns and I am on my knees. The next day I am back at Sloan-Kettering. This time I sense an unbearable impatience in all the doctors and interns. They are sick of me. My infection has gone on too long and my body is not doing what it is supposed to do. After yet another CAT scan, it is revealed that the drain for my abscess is not in the right place. It cannot reach the remaining pool of spill. They will have to go into the wound again with another needle/tube. The second time a woman doctor fails to give me enough medication, and only the nurse seems to hear my screams. I return home, but it is clear that the abscess is swallowing me. I am no longer sure I can go the eight rounds. Vomiting in a cup in the back of a cab, I return to the hospital. Once there, we wait nine hours in the emergency room.

I am sick with hunger and they give me the approval to finally eat something. I am swallowing the first bite of salad when a nurse-practitioner arrives and starts screaming that I have totally messed up my chances of having surgery on the abscess. Lu tells her she doesn't have to be so punitive. Perhaps she hasn't noticed that I'm sick? This is the sister who has spent the last thirty years working to save AIDS babies, who has given her days to early child care in the poorest neighborhoods. This is the sister who knows that what happens at the beginning of your life determines everything. You don't mess with Lu. The nurse-practitioner leaves and comes back about ten minutes later in a total 180. She tells us they are ready to do the surgery. I am panicked now, not sure if she was lying about the procedure before or if she has now decided to kill me in order to punish my sister. Either way, it doesn't look good and it isn't. This time there is a new, youngish, inexperienced, almost handsome doctor who has clearly been called in for this procedure just as he was leaving for

the day. He's at the bottom of the food chain and has
no choice, but that doesn't mean he's friendly. He
clearly has dinner plans and my stinky elusive pool of
pus is holding him up. I sense immediately that he
hasn't done this abscess-incision-drainage thing much,
maybe never. The nurse on duty is older and she knows
more, but he isn't listening. I find myself whispering,
trying to explain that this is the third procedure and
they have all been very painful. I have regressed and
am suddenly ten years old, a whispering girl voice
pleading for mercy and drugs. He doesn't seem to hear
me, but the nurse does and she scrambles to get some
medication into me before late-for-dinner begins. I am
weak and infected, and my resistance is gone. It feels
like he is shoving a garden hose through my wound,
and now noise is coming out of my mouth. I am screaming, truly screaming. The nurse is kind and takes my
hand. "Stop. Please. Stop. It's too much. It hurts too
much, hurts. Stop." He does not pause. "Please drugs.
Give me drugs. This is too much. Really. Please. It
hurts." I am screaming, crying, begging. The nurse
tells me she has given me ativan. I tell her I know ativan. It will take too long. She shoots more of something
into me. I have no idea what it is, and I am sure that in
her panic she is overdosing me. Screaming. Stop. Stop.
He just keeps shoving the garden hose deeper into my
infected center. Deeper and deeper. He might as well

put his hand over my mouth. He might as well tell me not to scream, not to tell. He might as well remind me I am not even really there. It goes on forever, me screaming, him shoving the needle attached to the long thick tube. Then he is done. Abruptly he makes some final adjustments, takes off his radiology gown, and, without even looking at me, walks out. I lie there on the table, stunned, achy, bruised, and raw. I know these bruises. I know this stunned moment after.

All the nurse does is gently touch my hand and I begin to wail.

The next morning and half the day I do not move or speak. I lie in bed, floating in depression, methodically planning my funeral. It is dull and uninspired. Even I would not attend. Suddenly Toast appears in my bedroom. I am irritated. He says it's Mama C on the phone from the Congo and it sounds important. I know what he's doing. I put on my best activist voice, but Mama C can tell I'm a mess. She apologizes for even calling, but I can tell she's rattled. No one has seen the City of Joy building contractor for days and the workers have not been paid. There is about to be a huge strike and it will not be pretty. She needs me to call UNICEF. My self-hatred flips to rage in about half a second and I call Kinshasa. I am shocked at the anger in my voice and the pitch. I am raging at the institutions with the money and the glory, raging at the institutions that are meant to heal and support the sick and suffering but don't even see them. Raging at the indifference and trained neutrality of the powerful. Raging at the distracted oncologist, the blaming radiologist, the rock-and-roll catheter surgeon, the sadist-late-for-dinner doctor dude, the bruises all over my arms from over-worked and underpaid, bitter nurses. But it's Sloane-Kettering. And this is the best, it's Sloan-Kettering— where getting the best means you can't complain and you have to show gratitude for something you never received.

In my rage my energy returns, and I am back on my feet, back in the ring. Just what Toast had contrived.

I pace my room. I am smelly and ripe. I strip off my clothes. I look at myself naked in the mirror. I put my hand on my new bag and I watch the pus draining out of me. On my other side is my ileostomy bag and my poop. It seems impossible that within a few months all this has happened. I am so very sickly, skinny, but there is some crazy light in my eyes. I am fighting for my life. My bags are holsters. Inside are guns instead of pus and shit, and I pull them fast and aim-bang-fire Sloan-Kettering.

STAGES/5.2B

In the twenty years I have known my internist, Dr. Katz, he has never made a house call, so it is a great surprise when he magically appears in my loft. He takes one look at me and tells me I have lost at least thirty pounds and he is seriously worried. He insists I go back to the Mayo Clinic or to Beth Israel in New York, where he is connected. At Beth Israel I see Dr. Koulos, a super skinny man from the Midwest. He is caring, in a serious way, concerned, and to the point. There is something androgynous about his skinniness and that makes the pelvic exam seem less invasive. It is the first exam since the surgery and I am tense, very tense. He is gentle. I cannot even imagine what it looks like up there. Then he brings in Dr. Shapiro. They are friends of Dr. Katz, and I like them both. They actually look at me when they speak. Dr. Shapiro outlines my suggested treatment. He says there is no cancer now in my body.

The treatment is preventative. That is a good thing. He says it is a quickly growing cancer and they need to start soon. They hope my abscess infection will be gone by the end of the week. He says they are still debating whether they will treat me for stage IIIB or IVB cancer.

The words almost knock me off my chair. Stage III or IV cancer? Me?

They broke the rule. I had a rule. No talk of stages. I hate stages. The rule goes back to fifth grade when they decided in our upper-crust suburban middle school to institute a policy that would separate the brainy confident kids—the future Ivy Leaguers, and corporate presidents—from the sad, the slow, and the needy. There were four groups: 5.0, 5.1, 5.2B, and 5.2G. The highest was 5.0. I remember the day we received our assignments. In bold red letters, my card read 5.2B (which stood for *blue*, but I couldn't help think *bad*). It was as if the authorities had cast me as an idiot for the rest of my life. *Stupid*. There are many words that mean the same thing as *stupid*: unwise, thoughtless, ill-advised, rash, reckless, injudicious. None of them feel bad really. None of them hurt like *stupid* hurts. "Why did you do that? That was so ill-advised?" *Ill-advised* has a gentleness to it, but not *stupid*. *Stupid* is a word that gets into you, into your blood and your being. It gets into your cells. It is a violent word, a catastrophic word, a stigma, a scarlet letter *S*, and sadly it was my father's favorite word for me. Stupid. Eve Stupid. Stupid Eve. How did I make such a stupid girl? Is it possible you are this stupid? Could you be more stupid?

Everything I have done up to now in my life is to prove I am not stupid. I endangered myself many, many times to prove that I wasn't stupid, and that was even more stupid. I have pretended that I read books I never read and to know things I do not know. I never asked the questions I wanted to ask because questions indicated you were stupid, so in proving I wasn't stupid I reinforced my stupidity.

The worst group was 5.2B. We were not the ADD girls or children with speech disorders and learning difficulties. No, the organically challenged were 5.2G (gold). I think the gold was an attempt to make them feel special. Nothing they suffered was of their own making. The 5.2Bs were the wrong children, the fat, the pimply, the depressed, the painfully introverted, the ones with behavioral disorders, the broken and oily-haired girls, the aggressive, menacing boys.

5.2B was my prison. In some ways I have never left it. It doesn't matter how many books I read or write. It doesn't matter how many accolades I receive. I am forever marked 5.2B. Now Dr. Shapiro is giving me new marks, new categories, a new B for *bottom*.

Stage 0: The abnormal cells are found only on the surface of the inner lining of the uterus. The doctor may call this carcinoma in situ (again, 0 being where you want to be).

Stage I: The tumor has grown through the inner lining of the uterus to the endometrium. It may have invaded the myometrium.

Stage II: The tumor has invaded the cervix.

Stage IIIA: The tumor has spread to the outermost layer of uterus, tissue just beyond the uterus, and/or the peritoneum (membrane lining the abdominal cavity).

Stage IIIB: The tumor has spread to the vagina.

Stage IIIC: The turmoil has spread to the lymph nodes near the uterus.

Stage IVA: The tumor has invaded the bladder and/or bowel wall.

Stage IVB: The tumor has spread beyond the pelvis, including the lymph nodes in the abdomen or groin.

Stage III tumors have a five-year survival rate of 60 percent. Stage IV tumors have a five-year survival rate of 15–26 percent.

The Mayo team, being more literal, determined me to be IVB (there was cancer in the lymph nodes in my groin). Beth Israel was seeing me as IIIB. Either way, it was all Bs again. All bad.

There is something so dull and brutal about data.

Stage IVB cancer survivor, rape survivor. But I am not data and I don't want to be dismissed and judged by categories or grades. Tell someone you were raped and they move away. Tell someone you lost your money and they stop calling. Tell someone you have become homeless and you become invisible. Tell someone you've got cancer and they are terrified. They don't call. They don't know what to say. What if our understanding of ourselves were based not on static labels or stages but on our actions and our ability and our willingness to transform ourselves? What if we embraced the messy, evolving, surprising, out-of-control happening that is life and reckoned with its proximity and relationship to death? What if, instead of being afraid of even talking about death, we saw our lives in some ways as preparation for it? What if we were taught to ponder it and reflect on it and talk about it and enter it and rehearse it and try it on?

What if our lives were precious only up to a point? What if we held them loosely and understood that there were no guarantees? So that when you got sick you weren't a stage but in a process? And cancer, just like having your heart broken, or getting a new job, or going to school, were a teacher? What if, rather than being cast out and defined by some terminal category, you were identified as someone in the middle of a transformation that could deepen your soul, open your heart, and all the while—even if and particularly when you were dying—you would be supported by and be part of a community? And what if each of these things were what we were waiting for, moments of opening, of the deepening and the awakening of everyone around us? What if this were the point of our being here rather than acquiring and competing and consuming and writing each other off as stage IV or 5.2B?

My mind is reeling. Dr. Shapiro is still talking. I cut him off. "If the cancer is already gone, is chemo really necessary?" He says the line, "It only takes one cell." But won't there always be one cell? How will the chemo know to obliterate every single bad cell unless it obliterates every cell? If it obliterates every cell, how will I stay alive?

INFUSION SUITE

After meeting with Dr. Koulos and Dr. Shapiro, we were taken on a tour of the chemo ward, otherwise known as the infusion suite, which makes it sound like some high-end tea salon or aromatherapy spa. It was not. There were old people and sick people and bald people and dying people, and now I was one of them. I did not want to be one of them. I tried not to stare. Some were reading, others eating, some gazing into space, some dozing as tubes of poison pumped toxic carboplatin/Taxol/fluorouracil/doxil into their bloodstreams. The people who were by themselves seemed especially lonely. But what devastated me was their quiet, sad surrender. Suspended in their isolated comfy chairs, covered in little blankets, they were without protest, being carried to their end. I wanted to scream, "Hello. I see you. We need to talk. We can fight. We are in this together." I felt like I did in high school when I tried to organize all the unpopular girls. I called Linda C and Peggy S and invited them to my house. I said, "Let's face it, girls, we're unpopular. Let's form our own group. Let's take back the power." (I am not sure I said anything like that, but I did have a plan.) It failed. Linda and Peggy were highly antisocial, which is why they were unpopular, and they had no desire to create an unpopular-girls uprising. They just wanted to survive mean high school and grow up and be someone else. They didn't even particularly want to be my friends.

The nurse Regina introduced herself. Toast and Lu began taking notes. "We suggest you get a port. A port? Yes, a steel piece inserted in your chest under the skin. We can inject the chemo directly into it. This will prevent your veins from burning and collapsing. Each session will take five hours. You will be closely monitored." "Does anything ever go wrong?" I asked. "Do people ever have seriously bad reactions?" "We watch very carefully at the beginning to see how your body reacts. If there is any problem, we stop right away." "But if it's already in your body and it goes wrong, how can you stop it from killing you?" "No one has died here."

She didn't know me. She didn't understand that my body couldn't tolerate these things. I would be their first death. Then they wouldn't be able to tell people no one had died. I would ruin their record. Then they would have to say, "Yes, one person, one fluke play-wright died within minutes of her first treatment. Her body was not disposed toward poison. And oddly, she knew it. She felt it, but she didn't listen to her instincts. Shame."

ARTS AND CRAFTS

I don't know what made me want watercolors and pastels as I waited to be strong enough for the chemo. Arts and crafts, like music, had always been a particular nightmare for me. I was completely devoid of talent. My sudden hunger for art came as a great surprise. My desire to paint, like my ravenous need for a hamburger, seemed to well up from some buried, forgotten place, shaken loose by the rearrangement of my cells. All I knew was that I needed to paint and I wanted anyone who came to the loft to paint with me. The last arts and crafts incident had occurred many years before. It was during the Reagan years when he declared that a nuclear war was winnable. I was with a group of women activists in the desert at the Nevada nuclear test site. We were part of a major national action to occupy and shut down the site. We were a small guerilla group called Anonymous Women for Peace. We did spontaneous actions, like putting warning stickers on war toys and plastic soldiers at Christmas, dressing up as the Statue of Liberty and standing for days on the steps of the New York City Public Library handing out fliers to prevent nuclear weapons from coming into the harbors of Staten Island. We got arrested a lot, poured blood on things, tied ourselves to fences, and made peace camps in city parks. We were all Manhattan/Brooklyn girls with barely an idea of how to assemble a tent. Our first night in the Nevada desert we tried but eventually gave up and collapsed in our sleeping bags on the ground, which was most definitely covered in radioactive dust, not to mention crawling things like snakes and scorpions. The next morning the plan was for hundreds of us to invade the test site, go in as far as possible, and sit down. This was highly illegal and dangerous. Someone had brought a whole batch of white paper plates, which inspired the idea of making masks, a project that became more complex when one woman suggested the masks be two-sided: lovingkindweareinchargefightingfortheEarth face as we were walking into the site, warriorangryyouwillnotstopusmotherfucker face when the police came toward us. We would flip the mask at the moment of confrontation. I believe there were crayons and markers and maybe even some paint involved. Clearly my sisters excelled in arts and crafts. I was embarrassed and para-

lyzed. In the end, a few of the more talented ones inter-
vened and made my mask. I felt like I had cheated. We
entered the site, all locking arms, our lovingwesave-
theearth faces charging forward. There were suddenly hundreds of huge uniformed Nevada state police,
with mirrored sunglasses, wooden batons, hundreds of
white plastic cuffs dangling from their massive belts.
We never had time to flip to warriormotherfuckers.
Immediately we were thrown to the ground, painfully
handcuffed, roughly dragged into huge outdoor cages.
They kept us there the whole day in the hot sun, then
put us in a bus and drove us for hours in the dark, still
handcuffed, to the middle of nowhere and dumped us
there.

So here I was, years later, at my dining-room table
with paints and brushes.

People who came to visit were awkward. What was
there to say? Right away I would ask them to draw or
paint something with me. It worked like a charm. The
idea of making art often traumatized them more than
my cancer did. It turns out I wasn't the only one humiliated in third grade by arts and crafts. They would
start off grudgingly and terrified, but then they would
get into it. I began to love this new way of communi-
cating. My friends would sit by me and we would create together. It was quiet and communal. We were
children. People began to paint images of my healing.

Well, I asked them to. I hung these pictures on the wall and they became colored flags heralding the new country I was traveling toward. I was still weak and simply terrified by the idea of chemotherapy. I tried not to interpret the abscess as my body's refusing the chemo. I needed my friends and family. I needed their visions, their irony, sarcasm, and pictures. My niece Katherine made me a painting of all the foods I would eat again when I was better, sans bag. People drew all kinds of transformative things: butterflies and Buddhas and existential landscapes. In the first picture I drew, I was alone in a boat far out at sea, and there were storm clouds. Purva made a portrait of me that had no face. Something about it relaxed me. The shape of me was there, but my new identity had not emerged. Kim drew a many-layered healing mandala of the universe.

It was painting together that allowed my granddaughter, Coco, to begin to process the new declined scary state of her Bubbe. Coco is the closest thing I have ever had to a perfect relationship. From the moment she came out of her stunning Iranian/Irish mother, Shiva, and landed in my arms, we were one. Not merged so much, but joined, in affinity, in worldview, in energy, in lifetimes of connection. She is the female version of my son, has his eyes and freckles, but she likes to talk. Even as a baby she had a wicked sense of humor. She wanted to play and play and never sleep. She loved everything about people, studying them, trying them on. We had secret codes and stories. She once told me I was "her person" and she was mine. She was now thirteen and I could tell how much she didn't want to grow up—almost as much as I didn't. Together we were young. I feared sickness would separate us. It made me old. I was so scared that I would be the one to bring death and loss and darkness into her life. She would forever associate me with the end of her innocence. I would become Bubbe negative. But it didn't go like that, at first. She curled into my skinny frame. I was her Bubbe. She was not afraid of me, only the contraptions hanging from my body.

Coco and I spent a day painting and reading out loud. She played me new music and showed me Facebook shots of her many best friends. I was tired, still in the last stages of infection. I got weaker, but I pushed myself and ignored it. I wanted Coco to see me strong. I wanted to be well for her. More people arrived: Katherine, my niece who looks identical to my mother, and James, who everyone thinks is my brother. By then my performance skills had failed. I could not move from the couch and I was beginning to look green. That's when they called my sister.

By the time Lu arrived I had a high fever and I was

fading fast. She went into Lu action and called doctors and arranged a car to take me to the emergency room. As they were carrying me out the door, I could hear Coco wailing in the background. Shiva was trying to comfort her, but she was inconsolable. I suddenly knew why it was best not to attend your own funeral.

THE ROOM WITH A TREE

I was in the Beth Israel emergency room much of the night with Lu, Toast, Katherine, and my niece Hannah. We waited in the midst of violent quarrels, bloody knife wounds, premature labor, and serious drug overdoses. At around three in the morning I was moved to a hospital room on a loud floor. Lu sat by my bed in a very uncomfortable-looking chair, nodding on and off the whole night. I watched her sleeping. Why was she here? What had changed? Then, somewhere around five in the morning, it hit me. She was here because she could be here. All the years she had been forced to be a witness of my abuse, she could do nothing. She had been made to feel somehow complicit by her powerlessness. This would not happen again. Now she could fight for me. Now she could help me. Now she could be my fiercest advocate, my strongest defender. This had been my dream, that she would stand up for me, that she would reveal her love, that she would say that I mattered to her.

I was quite sick in the morning, unable to eat, nauseous, completely fatigued. I seriously doubted this infection was ever leaving. Toast came early with Coco and Shiva. Coco immediately climbed into my bed and wrapped herself around me. I think she just wanted to make sure I was breathing. Lu had heard about a new section of the hospital, and Coco went with her to check it out. They came back excited. My birthday was in a few days and this was a place where I could be quiet and celebrate. I would get better there. And the nurses seemed really kind. At first I balked at the private room, but my sister insisted, saying that my mother wanted to pay for it. I am sure she made this up, but the idea that my mother wanted to take care of me in any way was so miraculous, I accepted.

So here's my confession: My whole life I dreamed of hospitals. I wanted a washcloth on my head, my bedpan changed, and a kind, doting face worrying over me. Hospitals were the set location for many of my daydreams and sexual fantasies: doctors who were tending me, suddenly seducing me, their care leading to their attraction and inability to contain themselves, or nurses who while taking my temperature had no choice but to start making out with me. I know there are people who hate hospitals. I am not one of them. When everything gets exhausting in my brain and I cannot imagine going on, I put myself in this pristine, fresh room with sunlight and loving people in starched uniforms. And now out of nowhere, my dream was coming true.

The room was the room of my dreams. It was clean and pretty. All the machinery was there, but it was human. There was a couch that pulled out for sleeping and a small kitchen and a window right in front of the bed. What I hadn't anticipated was the tree. I was too weak to think or write or call or even watch a movie. All I could do was stare at the tree, which was the only thing in my view. At first it annoyed me and I thought I would go mad from boredom. But after the first days and many hours, I began to see the tree.

On Tuesday I meditated on bark; on Friday, the green leaves shimmering in late afternoon light. For hours I lost myself, my body, my being dissolving into tree.

I was raised in America. All value lies in the future, in the dream, in production. There is no present tense. There is no value in what is, only in what might be made or exploited from what already exists. Of course the same was true for me. I had no inherent value. Without work or effort, without making myself into something significant, without proving my worth, I had no right or reason to be here. Life itself was inconsequential unless it led to something. Unless the tree would be wood, would be house, would be table, what value was there to tree? So to actually lie in my hospital bed and see tree, enter the tree, to find the green life inherent in tree, this was the awakening. Each morning I opened my eyes. I could not wait to focus on tree. I would let the tree take me. Each day it was different, based on the light or wind or rain. The tree was a tonic and a cure, a guru and a teaching.

"I never want to see another tree," I said with bravado at twenty-two as I was speeding down a turnpike away from the green hills of Vermont toward Manhattan. I think I said "fucking tree." I never want to see another fucking tree. It was a joke, but it wasn't a joke. I hated trees. They had come to mean small towns and small minds, isolation and gossip, long, freezing winters and endless, green, swallowing landscapes, skiing coeds and empty chatter, families and babies, marriage and life. Trees had everything to do with life. I drove that day out of the forests and hills and blue skies and nights of falling stars into concrete, after-hours joints, Mafia hit men, anonymous sex, anonymous despair, gin and bourbon, and an end to morning, let alone trees. I see now how much I wanted to die, or how much I did not want to live with the pain inside me.

A group therapist once said that if you want to understand your relationship to your mother, look at your relationship to groups, but I say, "Look at your relationship to the Earth." The Earth was terrifying to me and separate, radically apart, foreign. I wanted it so much, I stopped wanting it.

This tree outside my room brought back other trees, trees I had seen without seeing, had loved without loving: the weeping willow at the bottom of my driveway in Scarsdale, madly shedding in the fall, making a shimmering bed of soft white lime leaves; the majestic pine trees in Croatia by the sea, filled with vociferous cicadas in late summer; the single tree in the middle of the Mara in Kenya, the lonely solitary tree that I first sat under with a beaded Masai mother who had stopped the practice of female genital mutilation on her daughter and kept playfully punching my arm with joy; the tree in Kabul, or I should say the stump of an ancient tree that had been cut down and burned by rebels, and the way the old, very wrinkled caretaker of the park cried when he talked about the hundred-year-old tree becoming firewood for some wild men for a few stupid nights.

I had days of silence with my tree and my dear friend and Paris neighbor, MC, who came to stay with me in the hospital. She is Belgian and the quietest person I know. Her silence was new like the tree. At first it was disconcerting, then, over time, delicious. Her presence did not require me to do anything: not to explain or entertain or make sense. She did not ask for anything, and she did not invade the boundaries of my illness. There was a week of silence, of presence, of tree. There was another CAT scan. There was a decision not to touch the tube but trust that the infection would leave. The approach was more nuanced at Beth Israel, mainly because they seemed to have time. There were visits from the oncologist. There was an outrageous birthday party in my room, which felt like a Hare Krishna scene. Deirdre did a healing ritual. Several of my women friends and Toast showered me with rose petals and oils. There was chanting. There was Lu trying to go along with it, rolling her eyes, hating every minute. There was red quinoa made by Bassia that tasted like the bloody beet-filled Earth. There was a wonderful cake. There were many presents, most of them soft and colorful pajamas and nightgowns. It was a mystical party in the wondrous room and there was the tree. My tree. Not that I owned it. I had no desire for that. But it had come to be my friend, my point of connection and meditation, my new reason to live. I was not writing or producing or on the phone or making anything happen. (Okay, I did make calls to the Congo every day.) I was not contributing much more than my appreciation of tree, my love of green, my commitment to trunk and bark, my celebration of branch, my insane delight over the gentle white May blossoms that were beginning to flower everywhere.

A BUZZ CUT

In India, head shaving is practiced by many Hindus and seems to have more ritual significance than any other kind of hair removal.

At first I think we will do a head-shaving ritual. I will invite all my friends and I will take the bodhisāttva vow. I imagine bowing down, humble, bald, stripped, away. But in the planning, the whole thing feels a little over the top and not so humble. Then my friend Sonja, who is super hot with a shaved head, tells me about her Italian barber on Tenth Avenue who charges only twelve dollars, and it seems so straightforward. So I go with Toast, Paula, Sonja, and Sonja's lover, Claire, to an old-fashioned New York City barbershop. A whole group of Italian men debate my hair. Two of them wonder why I would want to get rid of it, and one super fit sexy man with a tattoo and shaved head keeps saying, "Go for it." I don't say I just had cancer, it's not a choice, or that I don't want to wake up in the middle of the night with Silkwood clumps in my hand and bald patches in my scalp. I don't say that this is a kind of eviction from a hairstyle that had become my home, or that my bangs and Louise Brooks bob were me. I don't say it took me a lifetime to find that haircut and I swore I would never change it, or that when I was ten the boys in my class stripped me and called me "seaweed hair" because my hair was stringy and oily and pointless, and that having lousy hair was more painful than being half naked in front of most of my class.

And before I can say an absolute yes, Antonio is suddenly standing behind me with loud boy 4 clippers that are moving very close to my head. It never occurred to me that he would begin with my bangs—the fringe, the curtain, the veil. In less than a minute—gone. I watch Paula taking pictures of clumps of my dyed-black hair like little animals on the barber's floor.

Some people think I look sexy with a shaved head. Some say I look like a boy and it turns them on. Some get that I'm sick and this is not a hairdo at all. Many think I look like a dyke. I feel exposed. Present. Humble. Clean. Clear. I don't have to DO ANYTHING . . . with my hair. It is not who I am. I am suddenly face. All face.

GETTING PORT

There is something about getting anything foreign inserted into the body that is both downright creepy and fabulously supernatural. It didn't hurt; they were careful at Beth Israel. I was wide awake and I could feel the knife slitting the opening of my skin right under my collarbone, making a kind of pouch for my new port. Port. Port. All week I'd been saying the word. "Friday I will get my port." "This week they will insert the port." The port was to make chemo easier. It was a steel piece, like a pendant, that was placed under my skin and lived in my body. It had a tail, which was a tube where the chemo flowed into my blood. Veins filled with poison like Taxol and carboplatin can collapse and burn. My veins were elusive anyway. After weeks of poking and prodding and slapping, who could blame them? The port eliminated the anxiety of yet another search for veins. They put the needles directly into the port.

When I thought *port*, I thought *water*. I thought *ocean*. I thought *summer*. I thought *harbor*. I thought *ships* and *cargo*. But mainly I thought of leaving, of departure. Funny, I did not think *arriving*. From the moment the steel port was inserted into my flesh, I knew I was being taken somewhere. I was a passenger with a port. The port was the fixed spot, where the chemical load could moor itself and enter me. I couldn't stop touching it. It was lumpy and scary at first. I could literally feel the steel rising under my skin. I started to like it. It became a talisman and a weapon. I showed it off at dinners, flashing it to people who seemed severely privileged and ungrateful. They were so horrified they stopped whining, at least with me. A hard foreign object under the skin separates you from those who remain only flesh. It gives you secret powers and access to a new world, a world where there are no more countries or claimed borders, where life happens and death is near, where the only real harbors are the ones we carry in our chest.

THE CHEMO ISN'T FOR YOU

The day before chemo, Lu surprises me with a wall-size photograph of Muhammad Ali, the moment after he knocks out George Foreman in Kinshasa. It's one of those almost impossible photographs where time has stopped—Ali is standing, Foreman is on the ground. Ali has clearly won, but it's not the glory that hits you, it's the shock and the stagger of the struggle. It's clearly one second before Ali realizes he is champion, and you can imagine him a moment later prancing around, raising his gloves, bragging and celebrating. But here he is dazed and empty. Toast and I hang the photo on the wall and it becomes a kind of visual mantra board. I will turn to it many times a day over the next months. Ali is me. Foreman is my cancer.

I watch Toast arranging my chemo pills in our new purple pill tray box. He is parceling out the capsules

like Pez, doing it so perfectly and exactly. Monday:
Emend, Zofran, Advil; Tuesday: Emend, Zofran . . . I
want to kiss him.

Then Sue arrives. She has not been my therapist for
many years. We are post-therapy friends, which means
we have dinner occasionally in vegetarian restaurants
and talk about death and trauma. I call her when I have
insufferable anxiety or when I need a reminder that my
self-hatred is really massive anger. She heard from a
friend that I had cancer and is giving me free sessions
as a gift. I can hardly believe it. I can tell she is pretty
shocked to see me. I am super skinny and wobbly, with
a buzz cut. We sit on the couch, a stunned Ali as our
backdrop. Sue was the shrink I finally found after all
the others. I first saw her when my marriage was falling apart. I had just come back from a trip to Germany
where the Berlin Wall was coming down. The first
night in Germany I had a terrifying dream. My father
was raping me with an object and my mother was
calmly watching. I woke up screaming. This was after
ten years in New York City therapy with two different
shrinks, both telling me, like Freud, that everything I
thought happened with my father was just my fantasy.
Sue was the first person who was not afraid of my
memories. When I told her my dream, she said, "It

could be a dream, Eve. But sometimes dreams are also memories. I sense you have been terribly abused. I think I can help you."

Sue was a psychic surgeon who reattached shards of body sensations to memories. She had never been in my loft and it never occurred to me she would ever sit on my couch or actually touch my things. Shrinks live in offices.

"Tell me everything," she says. I start to cry. "I have been very sick. There was a huge operation and then an infection. Now they are going to poison me. I do not think I can do the chemo. I am not good with things in my body. It's why I never did ayahuasca in the rain forest. I knew I would embarrass myself in front of the shamans and the elders. I don't do well vomiting. I could never be a bulimic." I remind her I am totally claustrophobic.

Sue tells me that she has never understood how I have not been sick before. She tells me she knows I will survive everything because I am the most resilient person she's ever known. It's funny, I feel different when she says this, maybe because I know she knows how fragile I am. Then she tells me that ever since she heard about my cancer, she's been thinking much more about how my father battered me, and I say, "Me too." She says,

"I feel we didn't spend enough time on the battering."
And this makes me think of the chemotherapy battering my insides. I tell her I am very afraid of having
poison inside me. And then she does what I call a Sue.
She gives me back the same information I am giving
her but with a genius spin, a way of seeing things that
immediately and spontaneously unlocks the neurosis.
In this case, she gives me a way to reframe the entire
chemo experience. She says, "The chemo is not for
you. It is for the cancer, for all the past crimes, it's for
your father, it's for the rapists, it's for the perpetrators.
You're going to poison them now and they are never
coming back. Chemo will purge the badness that was
projected onto you but was never yours. I have total
faith in your resilience and the magical capacities of
your body and soul for healing. Your job is to welcome
the chemo as an empathetic warrior, who is coming in
to rescue your innocence by killing off the perpetrator
who got inside you. You have many bodies; new ones
will be born out of this transformational time of love
and care. When you feel nauseous or terrible, just
imagine how hard the chemo is fighting on your behalf
and on behalf of all women's bodies, restoring wholeness,
innocence, peace. Welcome the chemo as empathetic
warrior." Consciousness leap, consciousness shift. I
think rain forest. I think walking into what the shamans

call "the frontiers of mental death." I think that what was terrifying and impossible two minutes ago is suddenly the thing I need to be doing most. I think yes, chemo will be my medicine. I will ride it like a lion. I will let it do its work in me. I know that whatever happens, will be what is required.

TARA, KALI, AND SUE

The day before chemo starts I am in bed holding a soft, multicolored pink shawl (a gift from Pat), almost petting it, and repeating Sue's words: "The chemo is for the cancer, the perpetrators, the rapists, not for you. The chemo is for the cancer, the perpetrators . . ." I find myself rising, slowly walking to the center of my loft, toward the window with the antique golden sari curtains. I lay the pink material down on the floor carefully, as if preparing for a picnic on a beach. I walk back to the bedroom and face my Tara statue. Tara, mother of all Buddhas, who appeared in a woman's body. Tara, who fights off danger, fear, demons . . . hopefully cancer. Tara, who came through the Buddha's heart.

I lift Tara and I hold her in my arms. My heart is pounding because she is very heavy and I am weak. I should wait for someone to help me but I can't. I carry her out of the safe nestle of my room and rest her on the out-stretched pink cloth. I need you now, Tara. I need you in the center of this space, this room. I lower her. I dress the pink cloth around her feet and make a kind of shelf. Then I find a turquoise stone and a medal and a collection of trinkets that friends have sent to make me better. These are my offerings.

I have spent a lifetime building altars—a very odd thing for an atheist. I remember being in Lhasa, Tibet, on the roof of the Jokhang Temple, almost twenty years before, and looking down at the prayerful throngs of pilgrims who had come from everywhere to prostrate themselves in front of the temple. Some had rugs for their knees; others did not. I stood there for hours, transfixed, as if this dance of prayer hands pressed on crown, throat, heart, kneeling, lying flat, kneeling, standing, prayer hands pressed on crown, throat, heart, kneeling, lying flat were the only thing I had ever wanted to do, the only gesture I ever wanted to make. This was not something I admitted to myself con-sciously. Before I lifted Tara I was too embarrassed, too hip, too feminist, to prostrate myself in front of anyone or anything, too angry, too empowered, too self-directed, too cynical. Now the *I* of me had run out. I didn't know how I was going to live and I needed strength and guides to walk through this chemo forest of claustrophobic annihilation, violent puking, six treatments, numbness, infection, death. Prostration: placing the body in reverence, to submit, to surrender. In many faiths it is used to relinquish the ego. In Tibetan tantric Buddhism they do one hundred thousand prostrations to overcome pride. In Islam, prostration has been known to overcome many diseases.

All the hundreds of cards and letters and e-mails I received say the same thing. "We have no doubt you will make it. You are a force of nature. Nothing can stop you. You will beat this, Eve. You're a fighter." I know people are trying to give me support and make me feel strong, but sometimes it makes me anxious. What if it just isn't true? What if I can't beat this or it has nothing to do with me? Will it mean I'm a failure and or a failed force of nature, like one of those New York City hurricanes that never show up after you've put huge taped Xs on your windows? What if this isn't about fighting? I mean, how do you battle your own genomes?

Then I remember Sue talking about burning and death and I know that I need Kali too. There is a picture of her that Purva brought from India a few weeks ago. Kali: I seat her next to her sister Tara. Burn it away, Kali, burn it away. Make it new. Take me to the core of holy destruction and death and let me survive your excruciating heat. Let me throw what isn't useful into your flame. Dissolve it there and make me new, make me whole. Burn off the cells that are compulsively dividing and subdividing. Burn off all the parts of me that create separation and division. Burn off the stories. Burn off my contempt and my self-pity. Burn off all the ways I get ahead of myself and try to get ahead of others. And Tara, open my heart. Make me one with all sufferers.

Mainly, take my fear. And please, make it funny. I do not know why I was given cancer, why I have a tumor the size of a mango that has fistulaed and spread and broken through walls. I do not know why I am stage IIIB, really IV.

I need you to take it now. Let me prostrate myself at the altar of your insight and mercy. Tara, Kali, and Sue. Prayer hands pressed on crown, throat, heart, standing, kneeling, lying flat. Flat flat pressed pressed down as far as I get get into the floor.

CROWD CHEMO

I arrive at the infusion suite with a posse: Toast, Lu, Paula, Diana, Pat, and Purva. It's like crowd chemo. There are way too many people and not enough chairs, and we are causing a stir. Toast organizes everyone into shifts. This will be the pattern for all of my treatments. It is an embarrassment of riches. Dear Diana, always the first to arrive, dresses in skirts that are so sparkling and flamboyant that the suite becomes a swirling circus. She rubs my feet when the Benadryl kicks in and my legs are filled with anxiety. Pat is always running between two things or groups of people and almost always arrives with a present. She keeps me connected to the world. Paula can never settle—every day someone in her life seems to be dying of cancer. Purva brings the most amazing Israeli hummus from the neighborhood. It is so strange to see people eating burgers and fries as they're being pumped full of poison.

Toast runs my life by iPhone, distracting me with daily questions. Lu finds the nurses when we have worries, takes me and the IV to the bathroom, and covers me with blankets.

There's still time to back out. In theory the cancer is gone, so I do not need this poison. It's overkill. I see Toast and Lu catch each other's eye. They quote the "all you need is one bad cell" story. I think of all those much more evolved people who cured themselves with juices and diets. As the nurses prepare me for the first treatment, I think of a documentary I recently saw about assisted suicide. The man in the film was dying from ALS and he was only a few days away from not being able to swallow. I repeatedly watched the part where he drinks the poison and then slowly dies. His death was totally mundane, almost relaxing. My death from chemo will not be like that. It will happen within minutes. There will be choking and green toxic vomit and writhing. Diane, a tough-talking nurse from the Bronx, senses my terror and ambivalence. She launches into a cautionary tale of a chemo resistor (with Bronx accent): "There was this patient who came in here with her breast literally hanging off from the size of her tumor. She was giving herself those fancy vitamin C treatments. After about two weeks on the chemo her tumor shrank and began to disappear. Then she tells

me, 'You see, Diane, the vitamin C is finally working.'"
Diane is hysterical, and funny people can get me to do
just about anything. Her partner is Regina, a woman
who is so much a nurse that you instantly stick out your
arm when you see her coming. They are kind and
weathered and know their chemicals and antineoplastic
drugs. It's always people. Dr. Deb and her enveloping
kindness, Dr. Handsome who walked around the table.
Dr. Katz who made a house call that saved me. The
nurses at the Mayo who took me for walks and bathed
me. Now Diane and Regina.

Regina has to stick a huge needle through my chest
skin to go into the port. And that first stab is so deep
and painful, it punctures my soul. I follow Sue's direction. This is my medicine and these women, Regina
and Diane, are my medicine women guides. There are
no trees in the infusion suite. There is no moon or night
sky, but the suite will be my rain forest. There are bags
of liquids hanging above my head—Benadryl and more
steroids. These enter me first and pump me with heart-
racing adrenaline. I am taking off. Then it's time for the
Taxol. Lu holds my hand. I take a deep breath and close
my eyes. I pray to surrender. I invite Kali's magic into
me. I visualize liquid fire coursing through my muscles
and organs and blood. I see it reaching deep into my
nodes and intricate fibers and cells. I see it going in
even deeper down to the archetypal network, down to

molecules of sorrow and self-hatred and pain. I ask Kali to let me be brave. I ask her not to hold back, to take me all the way. Suddenly my face is on fire and Regina comes, takes one look, and stops the Taxol. This happens, she says. The body gets overwhelmed at the beginning. Somehow I like this burning. I like my red face. I am an awakened warrior. I know Kali has taken root. I know now I have the women around me who will guide me through.

The whole ritual will take almost five hours. I will do this five more times. Each time I will close my eyes and feel Kali and her raging fluid. Each time she will ravish and char me deeper, and each time I will look at my fellow patients in their cozy bedlike chairs. The Dominican woman in her fabulous hat, the stunning Egyptian girl who looks just like her attentive mother, the twelve-year-old African American boy with his raging headphones, the elegant Waspy woman whose husband always comes to fetch her later. Some are dozing. Some are staring off. Many of them are here alone. I will look at their faces and know they are my tribe. I will say a silent prayer for each of us that our potions burn away our sickness and despair. I want to live, of course I do. But right now what I want the most is to be swimming freely alongside the others in this burning river.

THE OBSTRUCTION, OR
HOW TREE SAVED ME

I was flying through days one to three of the first treatment without even the slightest reaction, and I was a little spooked. It might have been the steroids that had me amped and busy cleaning out closets at two in the morning. Or the Zofran, a very effective antinausea medication, that had kept the side effects at bay, but suddenly on day four the chemo was in me, on me, through me. It began with mild skirmishes and then, within minutes, there was all-out body war.

Chemotherapy can kill cancer cells if it can stop them from dividing. The faster the division of cells, the more hope of zapping them and dissolving the tumor. I no longer had any tumor or cancer cells. The chemo was going after the *possibility* of cells: any lone soldier cell that brazenly began forming would be zapped in the act of creation, or commit cell suicide, something called self-death or apoptosis. I was lucky that my cancer was the kind in which cells did rapidly divide, the kind that chemo was most effective at killing. But sadly it couldn't distinguish those cells from the healthy ones. It attacked them where they grew the fastest: in the blood, the mouth, the hair, the stomach, and the bowels. My stomach and colon were already vulnerable from the months of infection, which is why on day four, my whole lower body shut down, literally. My stoma and the surrounding area had already proved to be highly sensitive and would swell whenever I ate the wrong food or was even a little anxious. Then I wouldn't be able to anchor the bag properly on the swollen surface and it would fall off or break open. But now something else was going on. Well, actually nothing was going on. That was the problem. My poop and my body had come to a complete standstill. It was as if my body had been scared into shock and had died, even though I still seemed to be breathing. I began to get sick, really sick, nauseous and dizzy and weak. My goddaughter, Adisa, and my niece Katherine, had volunteered to take care of their auntie godmother for the weekend. I didn't want to worry them, so I really tried to ignore what was happening, to eat things that would make the nausea better. But all that did was further clog the drain. My stomach began to swell around the stoma and I felt worse, sicker, vomiting and spinning until sometime very early in the morning I found myself crawling on all fours, moaning in pain. My bag was empty. Before I knew it, I was back in the hospital, strapped to an IV. I had a serious obstruction—an obstacle, a block, a barricade.

I was back in the room with the tree. This time I felt lonely and sad, deeply sad. Some part of me didn't want to cooperate or move forward.

The tree seemed to mock my self-pity. I was raging, I was totally exhausted by myself, exhausted by my desperate fear of vanishing into ordinary. I was at the end of my body's road. Everything had stopped inside me, even tears. I passed out.

When I woke up my bag was full and life, it seemed, was coursing through me. The tree had worked its magic. What I didn't know was that the tree was actually inside me and saving my life. It turns out that Taxol, one of my chemo chemicals, is found in the bark of the ancient yew tree. Even better, the Taxol is made from the needles of the tree, so the tree does not have to be destroyed. Taxol functions to stabilize the cell structure so solidly that killer cells cannot divide and multiply.

It was a tree that was calming and protecting me, fortifying my cell structure so it was safe from attack. I had finally found my mother.

I WAS THAT GIRL
WHO WAS SUPPOSED TO BE DEAD, OR
HOW POT SAVED ME LATER

It seems a lifetime ago that I smoked pot on my way to school, sitting in a tiny sports car driven by a huge guy named W. I would be wrecked by homeroom, starving for munchies by second period. W, the son of a famous sports star, and I had gone from being a rising football player (him) and an overly enthusiastic, slightly desperate cheerleader (me) to a stoned-out dealer and a hippie chick in about three weeks. The transition was seamless. I knew that W, who reminded me of Lenny in *Of Mice and Men* (those huge hands), had a crush on me, so I was happy to be in his car every morning, sharing his stash. For my sixteenth birthday he gave me a tin filled with an ounce of grass and hundreds of black beauties, which kept me awake for the rest of the year, compulsively talking and constantly licking my lips. I did better on speed than on pot, which made me paranoid, and I was already paranoid. When I smoked pot, all I did was apologize. I'm stoned. I'm sorry. But that didn't stop me. I loved arriving at school, stepping out of W's incredibly cool car in a cloud of reefer, sunglasses concealing my bloodshot eyes, as Janis or the Grateful Dead blared in the background, and wobbling onto the plush green lawn in my torn blue jeans and Frye boots. I had no desire to be present. I despised Scarsdale. I was an outcast from the get-go. Never pretty enough, rich enough, thin enough. Never having the right friends, house, or clothes. The '60s, well, really, drugs, freed me. I got stoned and stopped giving a shit. I see now it was a momentary solution. Drugs and booze saved my life until they started to destroy it. From the first drink something hard, taut, and wired released in me. I was suddenly fun and funny—the life of the party. I was that wild girl, the one everyone secretly thought would be dead by twenty-one. The one who always pushed the edge, drove the car too fast with no hands on the steering wheel at midnight, the one who dared the boys and, when they were afraid, led the way leaping off the high quarry ledge, the one who got drunk with much older guys in dark joints that no one else even knew existed in a place like Scarsdale. The one who dated Billy, the heroin addict who was at least seven years older. With his Harley and his cool black motorcycle jacket, he would pick me up every day and we would spend the afternoon at his house, Billy nodding off, me mad methadrine talking. I was that girl who couldn't stop having sex. Sex relieved the pain and I was almost always in pain, so I needed a lot of sex. My life was spent managing the pain. I did heroin the night before my French SATs and was still so stoned the next day, I drew a huge black X through the entire exam. I was that girl who got arrested for stealing a huge bag of sunglasses from Genung's department store in White Plains for my friends or my wished-for friends, in order to ratchet up my popularity. I was that sad, wild girl, who was clearly the outcome of something that had happened or was happening to her inside her house, but in those days no one knew the signs or would even admit that such a thing was even possible. I was that girl who ran away after my father found me on the phone with Beth Post, my girl crush, the most beautiful blond girl (also a theme throughout my life). My father went crazy, humiliated me on the phone, called me horrible names for hours, whipped my legs so hard with his belt there were welts, then told me he was sending me to a school for juvenile delinquents and threw me in the basement to sleep with the dog. I was that girl who took off in the middle of the night and walked miles in the dark (diving into bushes to dodge police) to the other side of Scarsdale, where I snuck into my best friend Ginny's house, up into her attic bedroom, and woke her up pacing, out of breath. I was that

girl who slipped out every week and drove with W and
his hippie friends to Manhattan to the Fillmore East
(with at least a pound of hashish under the seat) to hear
Grace Slick or Tina Turner. I was ready for anything. I
was that wild girl who never thought about conse-
quences. When I was seventeen and my parents were
out of town, I flew to Berkeley, California, from New
York and met Jimmy, the coke dealer. I spent two days
testing coke and did so much, I had no ability to tell
one crop from another. All I remember is eating a
cooked artichoke dipped in warm butter. I flew back
with a pound of pure coke (a thousand dollars' worth)
in the pocket of Billy's black motorcycle jacket, which
he had loaned me for courage. Imagine trying to get
through today's security with a pound of coke in your
pocket. I was a suicide girl on a radical mission to get
out—out of Scarsdale, whitebourgeoissocialclimbing-
shoppingmallstifling, out of my family, out of my
body—and drugs were the means of transport.

I was that girl in college who lived half naked, an exag-
gerated exhibitionist, an out bisexualalmostlesbian,
guilt-tripping and seducing every straight woman I
knew, sleeping with my roommate during the week
and with men on the weekends when her boyfriend
came to stay. I could never seem to land in either court.
My hunger for flesh and touch, breasts and penises,

mouths, love, and sex was massive, urgent, and indis-
criminate. I was that girl who became a bartender in a
redneck bar in Vermont and brought booze to all my
literature classes. I was the one who slept with most of
my professors and thought that was simply part of the
course. I was that girl who gave the commencement
speech at college graduation and spoke out against rac-
ism and sexism and then sat down in my seat in my cap
and gown and drank a bottle of Jack Daniel's passed to
me in a brown paper bag.

Later, when I'd spent all of the thousand dollars that
my father gave me at graduation (in about two weeks),
I was that wild girl turned mundane tragedy. I was that
girl who fell into my twenties unglamorously and compulsively promiscuous, drunk, and weepy, who ended
up working in a Mafia after-hours club sleeping with a
delicious-smelling hit man, waitressing in black tights
and an emerald tuxedo top with cheap diamond but-
tons. I was that girl who woke up one night from a
blackout to find Frankie, one of the good-looking Mafia
owners of the joint, banging my head against the bar,
ripping off my necklaces, while the other owners
watched without even thinking of intervening. I was
that girl who went out every night praying someone,
anyone, would finally put me out of my misery. It was
on the hard ground of the Old San Juan airport parking
lot in Puerto Rico, having just been beaten up by my

then boyfriend, eventual husband, that for whatever reason, and to this day it confounds me, I got down on my knees and swore to a God I didn't believe in that if I were granted the return of my mind, I would change. As I gripped the broken high heel of my shoe, and as cheap black makeup dripped down my swollen, drunken cheeks, I knew I needed to offer something huge because I had fallen so far. I was that wild girl who had totally lost my way, squandered my talents and gifts, alienated those who loved and believed in me, betrayed lovers and wives (an entrenched pattern born of an early love triangle—seducer father, perfect mother). I was that pathetic girl who had spent those central formative years frying my brain molecules. I had lost huge opportunities because of my arrogance, defiance, and righteousness. Putting down the bottle and the drugs was the hardest thing I ever did. At twenty-three I was sober, totally broke, and regularly visiting the emergency room at St. Vincent's Hospital in the Village with anxiety attacks. I didn't have a dollar to my name. I didn't even have a bank account until much later. I lived in a fourth-floor walk-up on Christopher Street for $120 a month and sold Avon to drag queens on the block. I taught writing in Harlem at a school for pregnant girls where full-bellied teenagers spent most of the class sucking their thumbs, trying to calm their poor terrorizedsoontobemotherwithoutaclueordesire nerves. I had nothing with which to self-medicate. There was no way to silence the avalanche of self-hatred, criticism, and fear that had been unleashed once I put the booze and drugs away. I was addicted to Tab and Vantage cigarettes and was a serious vegan, which meant I was eating pickled mushrooms and getting very little protein for my very troubled brain. Honestly, I don't remember eating. But I didn't drink or drug.

Now, thirty-two years later, pot was the way through chemo and I needed a way through. The most surprising people were instantly out copping for me. As most of my friends in my present life had never known me at my lowest or been with me when I drank or drugged, there was much excitement at coming over to watch me get high. It was theater. It was sport. I was suddenly a pot-smoking, meat-eating bald person with a bag. A holiday. Of sorts.

RIDING THE LION

Sue: "Ride the lion with all of the strength and love that you have found in your community. Although this anguish is very lonely, there is a new infant being born, in a community of love, protection, tenderness, and ferocious caregiving. We are all around you with our blessings. You are here with me. The life force in you is being released. Kali is being purged from your cells, so that your cells run clean of cancer, and your selves run clean of the projected not-you badness that has riddled you all of your life. Washed clean, you are finding your original goodness."

CHEMO DAY FIVE

Vagina pain, deep throbbing vagina pain

Crushing bone ache

Feet no longer feel the floor

Desire to die while you are at the height of fighting death.

Desire to vomit when you know the poison you want to eject is supposed to be saving your life.

Bag stinks of toxic fumes

Burning

Salem

Witches

Cells, exploding emoticons, committing suicide right and left

Loss of will

Exhausted but no sleep.

THINGS NOT TO THINK ABOUT ON DAY FIVE:

Global warming

Six million dead in the Congo

The pointlessness and expense of the UN

Garbage, where it goes

How much women spend on beauty products

Rush Limbaugh

Bankers

Health care in America

Friends whose cancer just came back

My mother's loneliness

C never calling even though I know he knows

BP

UNICEF

Larry Summers

Liberals

Republicans

Postracial anything

Afghanistan

Drones

Transsexual bashing

Polar bears drowning

Birds falling out of the sky

Climate change deniers

The bodies of decomposed women alone in the Congolese forest.

One cannot underestimate the importance of pot.

ON THE COUCH NEXT TO ME

My sister's existence utterly threatened my existence. I will never recover from the horrendous moment of her birth. I was already a scrappy two-year-old fighting for even the remotest glance from my blond beauty-queen mother. My sister could not exist. It was unbearable. So I made her disappear. I am not proud of this. She became a blur, a blob, a smear of existence—something that on occasion appeared out of the corner of my eye and then, with a blink, was made to go away. Of all the things I have done in my life, I am most ashamed of this. I have no doubt it is why I became a feminist—to somehow right this wrong. The concept of sisterhood was at such odds with the almost homicidal competitiveness that lived in me. Our parents, Chris and Arthur, sucked the life and air out of every room and party. Now there would be two of us fighting for what wasn't there.

I do not remember having outright murder fantasies about my sister, but I do remember the annihilating rage—a rage that once exploded in me so forcefully that I threw her under a chair and kicked her.

In the family hierarchy my sister was on the lowest rung. This both protected her and rendered her invisible. My father had all the oxygen, the resources, the money, the power, the charm, and the rest of us lived off the fumes. The closer you were to him, the more chance you had of breathing, but the proximity also meant serious danger. Who knows what makes each of us who we are. I got the idea wrongly or rightly that my survival was based on being heard, being seen even if it meant being abused and attacked. In securing the spotlight, I was anything but sisterly. Invisibility was the greatest enemy. This idea became the architectural framework of my life.

It took stage IIIB/IV cancer, a shamanic cleansing, and exorcising of the original narrative to allow me to begin to see that perhaps this story was not my story.

Of all the destructive things my father did—and there were many—nothing was as devastating and long-lasting as the way he divided us and turned us on each other. This was his deepest and most sustained legacy. I see how the division plays out everywhere, how this early destructive mutation of the family, just like that of a cancer cell, determines the psychic and social patterns of our existence. The world seems to be constructed on empires born of these mutations—of poor pitted against poor, ethnic group against ethnic group, elevating one group over another—a seduction that keeps the powerful in place. What if we weren't so susceptible to being the adored, the most, the cherished, the winner?

Now Lu was on the couch next to me, putting a washcloth on my head, rolling me joints (turned out she was as good at this as she is at everything), and reminding me to breathe, to take the Xanax, to stop reading the book on genocide. She had, it turned out, grown up and made a valuable life, devoted herself to her husband and daughter, done extraordinary work in the world. She had become a major somebody. And for whatever reason, she was here, taking care of me. I had been given a reprieve and so I shut up. I listened. I asked her questions and I was sincerely curious about the answers. At first I tolerated her substantial existence, but as the days passed I came to rejoice in it.

It was fragile, our new beginning. I was terrified of blowing it. I learned to be still, some days to do very little. I would be burning. We would eat a chicken, look at handbags online, play with her new iPad, cry at ridiculously bad movies, carefully and sporadically talk about Arthur and Chris. Lu had a threshold. I learned to respect it. I was not better or braver for being a trag-edy magnet. Lu's presence, her simple, soft-skinned, maternal-sister presence was a healing. My sister and I, on an island called Manhattan, with my body on fire, nausea racing through me, fell in love. That's the only way I can describe it. We found another direction for our attention, not up toward the impossible father or out toward the unreachable mother, but across to each other.

I LOVE YOUR HAIR, OR
THE LAST TIME I SAW MY MOTHER

I feed her chocolate ice cream and want to believe there was a time she did this for me. I have no memory of her putting food in my mouth. I hate her. Here I am, having climbed out of my chemo cocoon to fly south to feed her chocolate ice cream. Here I am, again taking care of her, hoping she might one day feel compelled to take care of me. An old shrink used to say, "You think if you paste arms on her, eventually she will hug you." I am shocked at my rage, shocked that she didn't pause when I entered her hospital room just now to say, "My god, you came. You flew here in the middle of chemotherapy to be with me." Instead, in her gradually descending dementia, she talks about how much she loves my hair. She has told all the nurses that I will set a fashion with my hair and it will be the rage in New York.

I have never set fashions. Most of my life I could

barely figure out what to wear. She insists I take off my scarf and I do because she is so ill. I want to make her happy. And she says, "I love it. I love your hair." I want to scream. "Are you looking at me, me, me? I am bald. Feel it, feel my head. There is nothing there. There is no hair. I have cancer, Mom. I just had half my organs removed. I have bloody poison in every pore and I could die and I am not eighty-five, I am fifty-seven, and I got on an airplane and risked infection because my white blood count is very low, I risked my fucking life to fly here for you, you, you." But I don't say that. No, I never do. I laugh and pull my nonexistent hair. Then she talks about my niece Katherine's long blond hair and stunning face, identical to her own.

She can't stop talking about my pretty niece, how pretty she is. I am bald and my niece is pretty. So pretty, just like her. Then she catches herself and says, "Oh, you are pretty too. You are all pretty," she says to the room, like "Drinks on the house," and I say, "I do not look like you. I never have. I am therefore not pretty." And this conversation feels so familiar, I crave the chemo antinausea medication.

Her long red fingernails look strangely out of place with her hospital gown. They are the only part of the invented her that remains. She is bone and moles and catheter tubes and bruises and itchy IVs. Her long white hair is so fine, it gets caught in everything. I think she is dozing when she says out of nowhere, "Guilt." My sister and I say, "What?" And she says, "Guilt. I am guilty that I did not love you all more." I lie. My sister doesn't lie. I say, "You have been a loving mother. There is nothing to be guilty about," and I think, What will this guilt do for any of us? Will it give me back the years I hurt myself and almost drank myself to death? Will it reverse the bruises on my legs and ass and neck from being choked and whipped and punched? Will it undo your taping me to chairs, putting underpants on my head for an entire day to teach me a lesson? Will it make me understand why you woke my drunken, raging father from his stupor to report things to him, things you knew would incite him to violence— "Come quick Arthur, she's at it again, she's smoking. I'll show you. Come quick. She snuck out with a boy. She's missing from her bed. Come quick, Arthur. You must handle this." And he did. Usually with his fists and curses, a half-awake, drunken, raging monster that you steered in my direction. Guilt. I lie.

I ask her if she wants to see my scar. She doesn't. She never has. I decide to show her anyway. The nurse who takes care of her pretends to be interested. I show her my scar—the entire length of my torso. She hardly looks and says, "Mine is so much longer. Mine wraps around my whole body." My mother does not have such a scar. It was just the same when she heard I had to have chemotherapy. She told me, "I had it. It wasn't that bad." She made it sound pretty easy. Then I discovered she had never had chemotherapy. I got cancer. Then my mother's cancer came back. Then I went to chemo. Then my mother decided to die. She will win this round.

She is so frail. She looks breakable, but she isn't. She has outlived everyone who believed she was breakable and treated her like china. She has survived three types of cancer. She said all the time, "I have no desire to live long. Let me out of here before I am that old." She is eighty-five and she is still fighting with one lung.

I rub her very bony chest and get her to breathe in and breathe out. I calm her down. I am surprised that I am able to do this. She is a child. I am her mother. I get her to close her eyes and then she leans her head against mine. I decide to talk to her through our heads. I decide to tell her everything. I decide this moment will be my freedom. I press my brain right up against hers. I tell her how angry I have been and I say it is over. I say, "I waited my whole life and you are not coming." I say, "I wanted to believe your wall would come down and you would remember me, and feel for me, and worry about me." I say, "This didn't happen." I say, "I hated you for this and I have carried this hate my whole life. I hated you because you did not protect me or teach me that through protecting me I had a right to protect myself." I say, "I got sick. I am done blaming you. It happened. It didn't happen. It was. It isn't. I want to be able to move on and not search the world for my mother and not crave adoration. I want this to be the moment where I get free, so I free you." We sit there head to head and I know that somewhere in there she can hear what I am saying, and I feel my body relax and my aversion and hunger leave me and she relaxes and we fall asleep like this.

I wake at 4:00 a.m. on a cot in her room and she is moaning. She is freezing. The air-conditioning is so cold and lonely. I take my blankets and climb into her bed. I wrap myself around her the way I always dreamed she would wrap herself around me. I enfold the blankets around her shivering bones and I pull her to me and I hold her so tight, her moaning stops. Then in her sleep she says, "I was having a terrible nightmare. I dreamed they came to take our hearts. They didn't want mine. They wanted yours the most. They are coming to take our hearts." I want to ask, "Who is they?" But somewhere I know. I hold her even tighter and I hear my voice deepen. I say,

"Don't be afraid. They will not get our hearts. I will not let them. I promise."

The next morning they move my mother to the cardiac unit because her heart has now become the problem. It is where we do not live that the dying comes.

IT WAS A BEACH, I THINK

The sun was setting. Lu wanted to sit outside. It was a beach, I think, but it might have been a parking lot. The wind was sea and salty. It was holding us and tearing things apart. There was nothing to say—we were past recrimination and longing, past who got loved more or who didn't get loved at all. Florida, the burnt place of fossils and remains.

I took off my hat. The wind blew through my sticky baldness. The humidity was an embrace. Lu and I were stunned at how fast it was all happening. My mother's dying made us strangely hungry. We ate things that children eat. Everything was fried. We shared. Lu had wine. There was a time when the silence would have pushed me to ask my sister to revisit the family horrors, but they didn't seem interesting now. The horrors. I thought of Lake Kivu, how once when I was crossing it from Goma to Bukavu, it turned into a raging

ocean, and the waves were higher than the boat loaded
with too many bags and people. I wasn't like the
others—worried about drowning. I knew I could swim.
I was terrified of what was under the water—all the
dead bodies and body parts—the people who had been
killed or raped or macheted in the forests, who died
with their families and whole villages so they were
never missed: the lonely floating bodies reaching out
in the dark water, bobbing like capsized possibilities,
still waiting their turn. I always thought I would die
walking into water. But I am not sure there was any
there, that night after we left my mother's room. It was
more the idea of water, the idea of something that
comes in really close and then pulls away just as you are
coming to understand it. It was my mother. The wind
holding Lu and me; the wind tearing everything apart.

SHIT

I remember my mother once proudly telling me that she toilet trained me in a week. I wouldn't learn, so she just kept me in my soiled diapers without changing them for six or seven days and she laughed, a strangely wicked laugh, and said, "Believe me, you got it. You begged to have those diapers taken off you."

Have I told you my mother was obsessed with giving me enemas as a child?

I don't remember being constipated. I don't think that is why she gave them to me. I think it was about cleaning me out, getting this thing out of me, this badness. I was born dark and Jewish and she was a Wasp. Well, kind of. She was part Wasp and part other things. Poor white kinds of things. Whereabouts and origins unknown. No one ever thought she was my mother, including me. I was convinced for a long time that I was adopted. When they discovered the hundreds of thousands of orphans in Romania after Nicolae Ceauşecu's twenty-five-year reign of terror, I was sure I had come from there. Enemas were my mother's way of making me something else. Perfect, French twist wrapped up tight—elegant, no mess. Enemas were about making me something that wouldn't embarrass her.

For years I was terrified of shit. I was plagued with dreams of shit, oceans of shit, swallowing and consuming me. Now I really was swimming in a sea of shit, shit I could no longer control. Now I was wearing a bag of shit, a swampy pouch of my unexpressed feelings pouring out at their discretion. This made leaving the house treacherous. Sometimes the bag just exploded. When I was anxious, my stomach swelled. The stoma glue couldn't hold and it was a mess. The bag could not be trusted if I ran into a person on the street speaking to me in the way that people speak to a person with cancer. You know? That sanctimonious pity that makes it horrifyingly evident that they have written you off. I smile that bald-headed smile and take care of them, tell them not to worry, I'm fine. Cancer free. Not going to die. But my bag is pissed off. By the time I've finished my bullshit sentence, the stoma is already beginning to swell, the bag filling up. Or, at a reading of a new play a producer I am having serious doubts about comes up to me, and as I go to shake his hand, I look down and realize my hand is covered in shit.

It was shit. Unpredictable shit. My shit and it was out there. There was no more hiding it or keeping it in.

RADA

I call my friend Rada with the red hair and the Yugo-slavian accent. Rada speaks fifteen languages and knows the history of every country, and if you point to a bridge or a monument anywhere in the world, she can tell you when it was built and why. She is a linguist and a feminist and an activist and makes the best vegetable soup I have ever tasted. She wrote the Finnish/Croatian dictionary. I need Rada. I ask her to come. It isn't just her soup, or her hands, or her skin, or her imagination, or the way she talks, or the things she knows. It isn't just that she is at once the brainiest and earthiest, or that she will be the one person who is not afraid of my bag or poop. It isn't just that. It's what we've been through traveling to war zones together.

I met her in 1994. I had seen a photograph on the cover of *Newsday*, six or seven young girls in a state of shock and terror having just escaped a rape camp in Bosnia. There was something about the picture, about the idea of a rape camp, that compelled me to find a way to get there and meet these girls. There was a place in Zagreb, the Center for Women War Victims. I faxed them a letter. They didn't respond. I faxed them again. It was clear they were not impressed. It was clear they had become cynical about journalists and writers coming from outside the country. I must have faxed four more letters and finally they agreed I could come and sleep on their office couch. I felt like I had won the Nobel Peace Prize. Rada was one of the women running the center. She was to be my translator, and it was clear she was not thrilled with the assignment. I was just another writer coming to steal their stories and leave them in pain. She was not enthusiastic, but she wasn't unkind, and she devoted hours to translating for me. We spent days in refugee camps and centers, backyards, and crumbling Communist compounds. It was summer and hot. We traveled in tight buses, sweat, trauma, and terror rising from the soaked clothes of the displaced and forgotten. That August we were engulfed in clouds of cigarette smoke and misery, drinking thick Turkish coffee and eating burek and baklava. It was in Bosnia that the women's stories began to enter me. Hundreds of stories of women dragged into public squares and raped in front of their husbands, families, and friends. Stories of young girls held for days like slaves, their bodies used over and over by psychotic soldiers, sometimes six or seven at a time. Stories where it was clear that rape was being used as an organized and systematic tactic to destroy Bosnians, Muslims, Croats, and, in some cases, Serbs. Stories of women being forced to leave their cows, goats, and fields, being forced to watch as soldiers led their husbands and sons away, never to return. Stories entering me like emotional shrapnel lodging in my cells and gut. Stories that would eventually own and direct me. Stories that would never let go. And of course these stories would lead to other women, other countries, other stories, all of which would eventually lead to the ultimate story that was the Congo. It all began here in Bosnia with my friend Rada and the stories I needed to hear, although I am not sure what I was seeking. I needed to know what violence looked like. I needed to know how others survived. I needed to listen. But what I really needed was to know the world, the truth of the world. I needed to find the invisible underlying story that connected everything. I returned to the Balkans again and again over the next years. Each time Rada was my host and companion.

This was how our friendship was forged—two women trying to understand war. Two women trying to love the women who suffered. We slept in tiny beds together, we shared fresh figs, we compared our runs and constipation, we got colds, and we cherished the places with good coffee. We smashed peaches, strawberries, cucumbers, and lemons in a bowl one day and made facial masks for refugees and survivors on an island. We did benefits and performances and workshops. We read books about trauma and took holidays on empty, abandoned Croatian beaches. We shared small summer cottages where we could hear each other fucking with our partners.

Now it was almost fifteen years later and we were both divorced after long marriages. There were new wars. Now I had cancer.

We went to Montauk, which is where I go when I need to disappear. We walked on the beach and Rada made her miraculous soup and we read poems out loud and showed each other photographs. We watched a video of the women building City of Joy. She dreamed wistfully of falling in love. I dreamed of surviving. We talked about war crimes tribunals and the Bosnian women still seeking justice. We talked about the conflict ending in the Congo. If my cancer disturbed her, I never knew it. It was another battle, another thing we would get through. There was work to be done. She fed my rage by feeding me news, she helped me make plans for the future, she rubbed my shoulders and my neck almost every day—pushing me, loving me, needing me, back, back into the ring.

DEATH AND TAMI TAYLOR

James stays with me for a month during chemo. He is the closest I have ever had to a real brother. We come from the same pod. He makes flower arrangements and paints beautiful pictures, organizes my closets, helps me get rid of old books. He builds me a Cat in the Hat bookcase and helps find the perfect glass door for my shower. Because he is an actor and an artist, he is very porous, and I feel somehow that we are doing the chemo together. Each night James and I move to Dillon, Texas. This is a surprise. I have never really been drawn to Texas or football or small towns. The nausea comes. The body aches. We smoke a joint, eat a picnic, and travel. I am not sure why or why now. I know Tami Taylor has a lot to do with it. She is tall with long red hair, supersmart, sexy, Southern, and kind without being stupid. I alternate between wanting her as a mother, a lover, and a friend. I live for Tami Taylor.

James lives for the totally unavailable bad boy, Tim Riggins. It's a TV show called *Friday Night Lights* that revolves around a high school football team. I have never really watched television before. It always depressed me.

What I love is that we now really live in Dillon, Texas. Our days are just marking time before we can be with our friends: Coach Taylor, Tami, Tim, Matt, Julie, Vince, Jess, and Lyla Garrity. I want to say it's not that their lives are more interesting, but in fact they are. I hardly leave the house, so this is the closest I get to traveling. I have become a person obsessed with a TV show. There are so many things I never thought would happen. Each day, some way in which I thought myself special or different comes undone. For example, I was convinced that I was not a "cancer person," whatever that meant. I thought cancer didn't happen to emotional people or manic people. I was sure I would die of a heart attack or stroke. What I failed to figure in was (a) *emotional* does not mean "enlightened," (b) the toxic world, (c) it was in my family, and (d) trauma. We make up stories to protect ourselves. I am not a cancer person. I am not someone who would die in a car crash. I had a rough childhood, so the rest of my life will be easy. I paid my dues. These little myths and fairy tales keep us from the existential brink. Now I had crossed over and had discovered that there are no rules or reliable stories. There is suffering. It is ordinary. It happens every day. More of it seems to happen the older you get, or maybe your vision for it just expands. It is as unavoidable as is your ordinariness, your baldness, and your bag.

TV always makes me think about death. There is something about the emptiness. I have thought about death since I was ten. Maybe even before.

I was ten and watching *The Invisible Man*, which seems like an extremely sophisticated movie for a child, and Claude Rains—who was my stand-in father, always so witty and clipped and handsome in that impenetrable kind of way—had thick, white, scary bandages around his face and head. In one key scene he unwraps them and I waited for the revelation of something hideous and grotesque. He unwraps the bandages and there, in place of some deformity, was something far worse. There was nothing, absolutely nothing where his face and head once were. Even now my blood chills and the nausea returns. Claude Rains was invisible, gone. I vomited for three days and right after became wickedly afraid of the dark.

Death. I have spent days trying to make friends with it. For many years I was plagued with something

I called the death thing—the sudden and acute realization of my own mortality, a complete flash of understanding that I will not be here anymore, gone. This flash is so immediate and so absolute, it takes my breath away. I have had the death thing in bookstores, in the shower, while working out, in bed. I have had it in my dreams and literally sit up with a gasp. It happened so often I could bring it on, which I began to do in an attempt to control or master it. Now I am in death. It is no longer a thing. It is not a flash of something that could happen. It is something that will happen. It is something that has already begun. I have a catastrophic illness. Many people die from it. I could be dead soon. People say not to think like this. But I wonder why or how I wouldn't think about the biggest thing that is going to happen to me.

Death is the thing that will end my existence and turn my body to dust or bones, and make it impossible for me to ever see the stars, or walk through the early days of spring, or laugh, or move my hips while someone is inside me. I think crying will help me. I will cry my way into death.

James sleeps next to me every night in my bed. We have never been this intimate. I am nervous. I am dying. I had cancer. My cells are trying to fight it off. It could go either way. I get up my courage. I say, "Jimmy" (I am the only one who calls him that), I say "Jimmy"—in a Southern accent just like Tami Taylor—"Jimmy, can I put my head on your chest." He says, in a deep man's voice, "Of course," and cuddles me in just like Coach.

A BURNING MEDITATION ON LOVE

There is something about the exhaustion of being poisoned, of your body fighting off the attack or just surviving the attack. There is something about being clutched, clenched, chemoed that is so deeply strenuous and catastrophic that it takes you to a mystical place where you are so deeply inside your body, inside the inside of the cavern that is your body, so deep inside that you scrape the bottom of the world. That is where I began this burning meditation on love.

I had been adored as a child and despised. I had been worshipped and desecrated. I knew nothing of love that was not based on conditions, love that did not involve living up to certain unrealizable expectations.

My father's heart had turned so cold, he was able to leave this world without ever reaching out to make things right or say good-bye. His heart had turned so cold that a week before he passed, in his delirious state, he told my mother to strike me from his will. (I was never clear why she told me this.) Then he told her to remember that I was a liar and that nothing I ever said could be trusted. When years later, I did the hardest thing I have ever done and went to see my mother by the sea to tell her my father had sexually molested me, she said she never would have believed me if he hadn't told her that.

Love was something you succeeded or failed at. It was like a corporate activity. You won or lost. People loved you and then they didn't. As with trees, I had missed the point. The men I, in theory, had loved and who, in theory, had loved me had all disappeared. After years of involvement, not one found his way to my loft during those long burning months. I received a two-line e-mail from my first husband of fifteen years, a card from a partner of thirteen years, and no word from another lover of equal duration. Later I heard he was insulted that I had not reached out to tell him I had cancer. No blame, just the facts. I had failed at love or at the story I had bought about love. As I rode my burning body down to the bottom of the world, I passed through the ghosts and glories of those love affairs—hideous moments and tender ones. Honestly, not much remained. No resentments, no longings. And that's what was most painful—to think that at fifty-six I had

come to this: no lover, no mate, and no nurturing memories. Despair burned in me. There were days when the
leaves of my romantic failings made a bonfire inside
me. The story I had been living about love was now
clearly over. The landscape was charred. There was no
way forward or back.

While this fire raged in me, some other alchemic
dance that I could not even recognize was happening
around me. It was MC cooking me soft-boiled eggs at
5:00 a.m. to calm my stomach, Amy who I hardly knew
stopping by unexpectedly to rub my feet, Susan appear-
ing in my hospital room, my son sleeping on my couch,
Nico coming from Italy for an entire month and turning my loft into a summer ashram, Nico shaving my
head with a pink Bic razor, Carole sending me weekly
boxes of silky pajamas, Jennifer walking me through
the dark nights of the infection, Donna spoonfeeding
me soup in the wretched Sloan-Kettering, Stephen
coming from Canada to take me to lunch and pretend-
ing I looked good when I was green, Michele coming
on Sundays to keep me sober, Avi and Naomi showing
up with pajamas and Bolivian quinoa, Cecile flying in
for the weekend, Jane arriving with hippie jewelry from
Woodstock, beloved Paula M finding her way to my
hospital room for my birthday, Coco packing my suit-
case the night before I went to see my mother, Purva
scoring me pot, Judy—who I have known since I was

four—and her daughter, Molly, my goddaughter, tag teaming me on some of the roughest nights, Kim sending me daily poems that seemed to arrive at the exact moment I needed them, Paula Jo photographing me naked with bags, the Sri Lankan girls sending a box of homemade cards, Mark walking with me into meditations on death, Bassia making me borscht. It was Pat contacting Dr. Deb and getting me into the Mayo Clinic, Laura and Elizabeth making me laugh, Urv making me dal. It was Lu showing up regularly with DVDs, and Toast, it was Toast with the devotion of Kent in *King Lear*, who gently kept me engaged and fighting. Always there. Never wavering. Never complaining. This daily subtle, simple gathering of kindnesses, stretched out across the chemo days and months was, in fact, love. Love. Why hadn't I known this was love?

I was always reaching for love, but it turns out love doesn't involve reaching. I was always dreaming of the big love, the ultimate love, the love that would sweep me off my feet or "break open the hard shell of my lesser self" (Daisaku Ikeda). The love that would bring on my surrender. The love that would inspire me to give everything. As I lay there, it occurred to me that while I had been dreaming of this big love, this ultimate love, I had, without realizing it, been giving and receiving love for most of my life. As with the trees that were right in front of me, I had been unable to value what sustained me, fed me, and gave me pleasure. And as with the trees, I was so busy waiting for and imagining and reaching and dreaming and preparing for this huge big love that I had totally missed the beauty and perfection of the soft-boiled eggs and Bolivian quinoa.

So much of life, it seems to me, is the framing and naming of things. I had been so busy creating a future of love that I never identified the life I was living as the life of love, because up until then I had never felt entitled enough or free enough or, honestly, brave enough to embrace my own narrative. Ironically, I had gone ahead and created the life I secretly must have wanted, but it had to be covert and off the record. Chemo was burning away the wrapper and suddenly I was in my version of life. Thus began the ecstasy—the joy, the pure joy of a spiritual pirate who finds the secret treasure.

I had always found the idea that we were meant to love only one person problematic. So forced. When I was younger, the word *monogamy* annoyed and terrified me. I refused to include it in my first and only marriage vows. I knew I was marrying a serial womanizer, so it seemed pointless, but also I was the one who had chosen a man who was incapable of fidelity. This relaxed something in me, took off the pressure. I was horrified at the idea of having sex with one person for the rest of my life. Now I see my fear was not about sex. It was about being caught, determined, lined up. It was about being cornered in the love stall. It was about packaged love, couple love, dead-and-done-with-permanently-in-the-house-with-the-children love. About love that screamed isolation and church and control. That screamed, "Care about your own, protect your lot." About parsed-out love and regulated love and pre-vented love.

I am not against two people loving each other, please understand—only the elevation of this love as the highest expression of love. Maybe love comes to some of us differently. Maybe we love our women friends as deeply or humanity as deeply. I am happy for those who find one person to satisfy their need to love. That has not been my story. I have not loved one man or one woman. In the same way I have not wanted MY child. I have loved. That energy that propelled me around the planet. I have loved some immediately and for a short time and others slowly and forever. I could not say that the men I ended up living with or sleeping with were more important loves. Those loves went on longer, in a more organized, committed, daily way. That was a good thing and not a good thing. Love is ever expanding and so it needs space, air, movement, freedom. I find I am much more loving when I have not made agreements about how I will love. It's like being forced to buy presents at Christmas—I do much better when I see something that reminds me of someone or when I feel a love rush and match it with a gift.

I have been afraid to write about this or even to admit it to myself. This is the way I love. I have no idea where it will lead me. What I do know is that when I am with the women of the Congo, of Bukavu, of Shabunda, of Bunyakiri, of Goma, I know love. I love Jeanne and Alfonsine and Alisa, I love Christine and Dr. Mukwege. I love the women on Essence Road who walk with two-hundred-pound sacks tied to their foreheads. I love the women who sell charcoal and fish on the open road and who dress in starched panges, so colorful they bring on the morning. I love the way they move and shout out and weep in sorrow. This is the big love, the ultimate love. It has nothing to do with marriage or ownership or having or consuming. It is about showing up and not forgetting, about keeping promises, about giving everything and losing everything. No one is mine. No Dr. Mukwege. No Christine. No women. They will never be mine. They were not meant to be mine. The world has done that already—possessed the Congo and pillaged her and dominated her and robbed her of agency and destiny. That is not love. That is possession, occupation. Love is something else, something rising and contagious and surprising. It isn't aware of itself. It isn't keeping track. It isn't something you sign for. It's endless and generous and enveloping. It's in the drums, in the voices, in the bodies of the wounded made suddenly whole, by the music, by each other, dancing.

MY MOTHER DIES

Lu has never spent the night before, but tonight she stays. Maybe it's because James cannot be with me, and I am in the hard days of the fifth treatment—aches and nausea and sorrow. Maybe it's because we had a conversation with our mother two days ago and she was speaking the language of the other world. There was a tenderness mingled in the muttering, but she was no longer speaking just to us. There were other beings, other spirits occupying her world. When we hung up we sensed that even Chris with her ability to fight off cancers and live with one lung, might not be able to wrestle her way back this time. Maybe Lu stayed that night because she and I were it—the family. My brother, Curtis, who had kindly surprised me and shown up at the Mayo, lived in Oklahoma. I had never really known him. He was the brilliant one, the seriously genius one. He read more books and knew more things than any-

one I'd ever met. He got an 800 on his physics SATS
when he was seventeen and I am not sure he ever took
a physics class. He had that kind of a mind. And he was
too sensitive to have had a sadistic father.

Lu and I slept in the same bed. We went to sleep holding
hands. At five the phone rang and our mother was dead.
We sat on the bed in a half-sleep daze and we cried, a
little, but it felt forced. We wanted to call her. To tell her.
How strange. We wanted to call someone else. But who?

My mother's body was sent to a crematorium. She had
left exact instructions as to how and when her body
was to be burned and how and when her ashes were to
be scattered over her beloved Gulf of Mexico. We were
not to be involved. There was to be no memorial, no
funeral. This nontradition tradition had been passed
on from my father. He had died, leaving us all grief
stumps. He forbade any ritual or gathering that would
indicate his passing. My mother and he never told me
he was dying, even though he had lung cancer and
faded slowly for months. When he finally passed, my
mother waited for some time to let me know. And even
then, there was nothing to do, no way to acknowledge
or confirm he was gone, no way to process the grief or
loss or come together as a family to determine a future.
This was the final act of my father's selfishness. He

despised people. He scorned the idea of anyone mourning him. Who would be good enough or smart enough for such a task? It never occurred to him that his funeral was not for him but for the people he was leaving. I remember flying to my parents' apartment in Florida after he died. I had not spoken to either of them for years. I remember spending time in my father's closet, sitting on the white carpeted floor, taking down his sweaters, his shirts, and his jackets and holding them. Putting them on. Inhaling them. His smell. Sweet, mean, and handsome. I remember raging at the mythology already being created by my family that he was an outstanding father and loving man.

I see now how, almost twenty years later, I have never really grieved his loss. He was there. Then he wasn't. I never experienced it as a loss, more like an existential magic trick. He was a man who adored me, committed incest with me, then regularly tried to murder me. Then, gone.

My father left this world without a call or a wave or a touch. This was his final cruelty. The last thing he could control was how my mother would leave this world. So many years after his death, my mother was still under his spell. He haunted her.

After I told my mother that my father had molested me, she called me one night and said she was very worried.

She asked me what would happen if she met my father in the next life and he was angry that she believed me. What if he felt betrayed? I said if by chance she did run into him in the next world, she could send him to me. "Send him to me, Mom." That's what I said. "Send him to me." This seemed to calm her down momentarily, but I have a feeling it continued to haunt her.

I funeral hopped for weeks after my mother died, searching for a way to grieve. I went to the funerals of my friends' parents and threw myself into their sorrow. I watched sad movies. I envied friends who were destroyed when their mothers died. I asked them to describe it to me. I took notes. I wanted to feel like something had been ripped out from under me. What I felt instead was longing: longing for grief, longing for loss, longing for it all to have meant something. I felt cold. A friend called to ask me how I was doing and I said, "It's day six of chemo, I'm exhausted, my stomach hurts, and my mother died." I said, it in one breath, just like that. My stomach hurts and my mother died. This numbness went on for weeks. Lu and I planned some lame rituals that never really came to be. She would call the crematorium from time to time to find out the status of my mother's ashes. They told her they were waiting for a few more urns to join hers so they could do one big boat trip out to sea. I imagined my mother's urn on a shelf all alone. I imagined her in something like a stockroom. I imagined the urns had handwritten labels, like jam. I wondered if there was some kind of religious person that went out on the boat. I wondered if he or she read the labels on each urn so they knew each name. I wondered if, as they tossed the ashes into the air (I'm sure they had the perfect way of doing this so the ashes didn't fly into their faces and hair), they called out her name. "We let you go now, Chris. We return you to the sea, to your beloved Gulf of Mexico. We leave you to rest with the dolphins and the crabs and the whales that you loved so well." One day, weeks later, they called to say her ashes would be tossed in the morning.

I remember one of the last walks I took with my mother to the beach. She was so frail, skin and bones, but even then she was still glamorous, dressed in bright white cropped pants and a turquoise shirt that accentuated her green eyes. She wore a straw hat that kept blowing off. I chased it for her. She held on to my arm as the gulf washed over our feet. We had the same feet and even the same red nail polish on our toes. She pulled at my arm, which was something she would do sometimes when we walked. It was as if she were trying to take me in another direction—perhaps in a direction she herself had always wanted to move, a place where she might have lived another life, one that wasn't determined by her fear of poverty or her desperate need to be fathered and safe. A friend of mine once told my mother that my father had four children, my brother, my sister, me, and her. He owned and controlled us all. I had felt this pull of her arm in mine on the beach all my life. This pull to save her even though on the surface she had no desire or willingness to be saved. This pull to give voice to what was mute and passive in her. This pull to live the life my mother had not lived. Now she was ashes. The pull was gone. And so was the boat with her urn. An overcast day. Loud seagulls circling. The water choppy. She wouldn't let me be there, but I am. I hold her ashes to the wind. I pause and say a silent prayer. Mom, go now, please, go, fly fly, fly.

About a month after my mother died, during my last chemo treatment, I went to New Orleans for the performance of a play, *Swimming Upstream*, written by a group of extraordinary women: writers, singers, Mardi Gras queens, actors, and social workers. It was the fifth anniversary of Katrina and we were preparing for a performance and a tour of the show. The women were so kind and found me a huge, comfy chair where I could sit and direct the play without spinning from the chemo. During rehearsal, Michaela, an extraordinary vocalist and a huge spirit, asked me if she could give me a healing. I was in need of healing.

Toast is with me and we arrive at Michaela's new house on an inviting street in New Orleans. The morning is gentle and sweet light is falling through her curtains. Michaela is busy preparing, mixing ingredients in a huge bowl in the kitchen. I am nervous, feeling vulnerable from the arduous and endless churning of the chemo, from my unwieldy bag, from being out in the world, and from the unfelt grief that renders me totally unpredictable. Michaela is concocting me something with flowers to make it beautiful, and honey to sweeten it. I ask her what is in the water. She says the Gulf of Mexico. The women begin to arrive. Carol B, heart of New Orleans, the Harriet Tubman of Katrina, Karen Kai, whose wounds make fire, Troi whose voice comes from all over her body, and Asali, whose word rhythms are cosmically inspired. The women and Toast surround me as Michaela lays me down on her lap. She cradles my bald head and begins to sing. I am finally a baby. She begins to gently caress my head with the water, with the gulf, with the flowers and the honey. And as she washes my head, she sings and the other women join her. I hear Toast's gorgeous, unmistakable voice. As Michaela washes my naked head, I realize this water holds the best and the worst of us. The greed, and the recklessness that led to the drilling explosion, and all the lies that got told before and after. It's the gulf that I swam in at the age of sixteen reciting T. S. Eliot's "The

Love Song of J. Alfred Prufrock." The gulf where both my parents died, their last gaze directed out on that horizon. It's the gulf, the wide hole, between my mother and me. The gulf dividing tribes, families, continents, and colors. The gulf washing over my head, melting in Michaela's lap, suddenly indistinguishable from my salty tears.

DE-PORTED

Deport: to force a foreign national to leave a country, to expel or banish someone from their own country.

When they put the port in, it felt like they had implanted a chip, an identification tag, a marker, something to track me and control me. As an anarchist who has spent so much of my life resisting all forms of authority, I was surprised at how comforted I felt by the port, an umbilicus connecting me to Taxol and carboplatin and Zofran and steroids and the infusion suite. I could lean back in my big chair when the dose got too strong and nod off in a chemo swirl surrounded by Lu and my friends. The port kept me attached to Dr. Shapira, to Regina and Diane, and to all the other patients who were attached through their ports in the chemo river, the river of possible cure. The port relieved me. It was doing the work for me. My job was to survive and find a way of imagining all this so that I could transform and tolerate it. My job was to find the poetry. Rather than making me feel sick, the port made me feel other and bionic. It made me feel superhuman, intensifying my strength and ability to survive. Chemo powered. Hooked up to my chemical mother. Sometimes at night when I would wake up with a gasp at the dreaded and vivid realization that I had cancer and that everything had changed, like the first nights in the Congo when I lost my way after the stories entered me, I would feel for my port like reaching for my talisman: a hard lump of steel, right under my flesh. I would caress it and calm myself.

When the time comes to have the port removed, the nurses are happy to see me and tell me I am the only person in two years whose port they have put in and also taken out. I know I have dodged a bullet. Lu and Toast are with me, of course. They are so happy that the port is going that they would be with me in the operating room if the nurses didn't ask them sternly to wait outside. I know they are ready to have this all behind us. I am not as ready. Chemo makes me feel I am doing something active to fight my cancer, makes me feel I am participating in killing off the bad cells. The port is the way I do this. Without the port I am vulnerable again. I am open to the cells dividing, disguising, invading. I am open to the destructive forces of proving and driving and fighting. The port is evidence that the chemo is in me. It is the place that holds five hours of Taxol and carboplatin mercilessly dripping into me.

Now the doctor sticks needles in me to numb where the port is, and it hurts and pinches and I hold the nurse's hand and I can sense the doctor making a slit in my skin. There's bleeding, and I can feel her dabbing it, and then she lifts the port, pulls it out of my flesh, rush of emptiness. I have become uncorked.

Trembling, panicked, I try to get dressed and hold back what is rushing through me until we get into the streets and then I let out a moan, the sound of a mother pushing new life into the world. A sob the sound of my mother gone. The umbilical cord that connected me to Earth, to land, to something tangible. Now severed. A sob, the sound of cancer, of death, of sudden life. A sob in the middle of Union Square. I can barely stand up and Lu and Toast hold me there.

Sue: "The question is not: Will you die? The question is which *you* needs to die off, so that the new self can live and thrive in a new, loving world."

LIVE BY THE VAGINA,
DIE BY THE VAGINA

I tried to explain to Dr. Sean that I have just had an enema and for some absurd reason they have scheduled my gynecological exam with him right after it and maybe we should rethink this. I am back at the Mayo, having a string of exams before the takedown surgery where they will remove the bag, as they believe that after months of healing, my reconstructed rectum and colon are now able to function properly.

It is the first time I have seen Dr. Sean since the chemo. My cancer has been gone almost a year, and as he was one of the Mayo surgeons who saved my life, I assume he will want to share in the glory. I slide all over his table, swimming in the enema waters leaking out of me, and I apologize. He tells me this is normal and I think, "For whom?" I resort to stupid overenthusiasm and say a number of dumb, impulsive things. "I feel great, I can tell it's gone, my CA-125 was a 4." Then I invoke my doctors in New York. I say, "They are talking of a possible cure." The minute I say *cure*, I know it is idiotic. Cure? What is ever cured? Cure is an indication that I do not understand cancer. *Cure* is a big word, an extreme, unsubstantiated word, a word that gets you dismissed. It indicates you are American and stupidly optimistic with a ridiculous candounabletoface-eternaldarkness attitude. It is equivalent to saying you believe in miracles or that you follow your instincts or trust your gut. *Cure* is an insult to well-disciplined minds and intelligence in general. Dr. Sean says, "I don't think we can think about a cure yet, Eve. We are quite a ways off from that. I think it is better we think more pragmatically." And then he says, "If it comes back, it will come back in your vagina, there's a ten percent chance. Have you thought about radiation? We can radiate your vagina." Radiate my vagina. I feel like a character in a futuristic sequel to *The Vagina Monologues*. Radiate my vagina. I hear him talking, saying something about beans, or beads, or beams of radiation in my vagina. They would insert them, he says calmly, easily, deliberately. Insert beans or beads in my vagina. Radiate my vagina. Do you know who I am? Do you have any irony? But more important, you just said *if* it comes back. *If* it comes back. You just stuck a long thick hat pin in my future. You just erased seven months of my getting through an insane infection, and weeks of chemo, and an exploding bag, and my believing and getting myself to believe it was gone forever. I need you to believe it is gone. Okay? I need you not to make space for it to return. Not in beans, or in your mind, or even in conversation. So take it back. Take the words back. My vagina heard you. Tell her you didn't mean it. Say you didn't mean it. You're my surgeon, for God's sake. You saved my fucking life. I worship you. Nine hours in my body. Cleaning out the mess. Don't give it away now. Don't sink me. Believe. I need you to believe. Oh my god. I really am a wuss. I refuse to accept or succumb to what some might call reality. I cannot tolerate bad news. I admit it. I hate it. I detest disappointment. I am weak—so be it. I know if I open the door, it's all over. That's how I've survived. Probably because I am totally suicidal at heart. I'm just not going down without a fight, okay?

I make good things out of bad. I always have. It's a kind of obsessive-compulsive disorder. In the end it probably is a failure of character: unable to face the utterly miserable heartless state of existence.

I know I had cancer, bad cancer, cancer that went to my nodes and all that. Stage III, IIIB almost, maybe IV. Well probably IV. I know all that. I know the goddamn percentages.

But it's gone now. Do you understand? It's gone. It has to be because that's how I am. I am a this-boat-will-not-sink-me person. I am a you-will-not-destroy-me-as-you're-whipping-me person. I am an I-will-find-a-way-out-of-this person. We all do what we do to survive. Cynicism. Optimism. Both paths require work.

You have to dig in hard not to be a believer.

You have to ratchet up your snark abilities.

Make bitter fun or be highly suspect of anyone who has faith.

It's not like I don't see the world. I am not in denial. No, I really see it. Then I work really hard to make it be something else.

Later Dr. Sean is kind and gives me some plastic objects of various sizes that he doesn't call dildos. He says these will help. It makes me happy that he imagines I will be having sex again. I hear myself ask him just out of curiosity what the side effects of beans, beads, beams in your vagina are and he says, all matter-of-fact, "Well, there are some not-good effects, the narrowing of the vagina, which could mean the end of intercourse, destruction of the bladder, severe diarrhea."

I weigh the pros and cons as I unconsciously grip the phallic helper in my hand. No more penetrative sex ever against a 10 percent chance . . . but destruction of bladder, severe diarrhea . . . Radiate this!

FARTING FOR CINDY

Toast and Lu circle my bed as if their quiet moving back and forth would stimulate my bowels. The take-down was over and the bag was gone. Everything was now about my bowels, my ability to control and direct my bowels. My bowels and our bowels. I was on the fart floor or the colon post-operation floor or the floor of missing bags. We were there, a tribe of us waiting to fart and poop. I met them in the hall, the middle-aged overweight male executive followed by his exhausted wife, the older, perfectly made-up buxom blond woman with a younger skinny man following her in a wake of perfume. There was a group of us walking and walk-ing, as we were told walking made you fart, made you want to poop. I saw some in their rooms still bedridden, and I saw others leaving, going home. Others who had clearly pooped their way back into the world.

It is terrifying not being able to poop or fart. Shit

claustrophobia—everything stuck inside you and there is no way it will get out and eventually you just explode. I was honestly scared: scared the operation had failed, scared nothing would ever work again and I would need another bag.

I could tell Lu and Toast were scared too. They were on fart alert. Each morning they would arrive with great anticipation, and I would shake my head. No farts. Not even a shot of wind. It was going on too long.

Then they sent me Cindy, the fart deliverer. She went room to room. She was very large, determined, and strong. The first time she came she told me, "Farts are music to my ears. I welcome farts. That's why I'm here. Do not be embarrassed. Give me your fart." I tried to imagine them saying something like this in Africa or Paris. It was so American. Give me your tired, your poor, your farts. Cindy knew all kinds of positions and tricks, places to press and pull. I surrendered to her big hands as she lifted and turned me about. I could feel she was gifted, but my new, redirected colon with shallow homemade rectum was having none of it. Cindy, fart massager, came every day at 3:00 p.m. I tried to imagine her life. Bringing down the fart. Finding the perfect place or exact right moment when the colon relaxed and the newly built body released. I honestly think it was my need to please Cindy that brought on my first slight pass of gas. It was her fourth visit and I could tell she was frustrated. She took her work seriously. Cindy was a volunteer. The fact that she didn't get paid for her fart work escalated my need to please her. If anything has kept my faith in humans, it is not the grand inventors or visionary poets or brain surgeons or even the Gandhis of this world. It is the Cindys, the quiet, invisible, often underpaid or unpaid Cindys who get up every morning, and after feeding their families, and taking care of their infirm parents, find their way on snowy country roads or polluted freeways to hospitals or old-age homes or mental institutions or orphanages. Frequently unacknowledged, they take care of the poor and the privileged, the sick and the depraved. They weave an invisible web of care through the lonely mansions of Beverly Hills and emergency wards and mammogram clinics and infusion suites.

As Cindy tossed me gently about, I thought of all the people like her who made me believe in love, the nannies and babysitters who helped me survive my childhood. Esther, who I met the first time I went to Panzi Hospital in Bukavu. I do not know her official title, but she is the Mama of the wounded. At any given time there were around two hundred women in the hospital who had been raped or suffered trauma and were waiting for surgery or recovering from it. Esther knew every single one of their names and their children's names and the reason for their fevers and rashes and she knew every detail of every woman's story. She created songs that reconstructed their narratives. Every day she danced with the survivors and played games with them. She transmitted her spirit into the broken and each day they got stronger. I thought of Miss Pat, who saved her church after Katrina so she could serve gumbo to the homeless, of Diane and Regina and the nurses at the Mayo.

As I lay there, Cindy had worked up a sweat. She was gently pressing my lower abdomen. When the world is right, it will be the unpaid and unsung people like Cindy who will be the honored ones, the ones who get paid the most, and they will sit at the big table. When the world is right, it will be these invisible people who we see and cherish. I open my eyes and I see Cindy's face and I know she is only here to help me get better. She has no other reason or agenda. She is so concentrated and so kind, I get seriously choked up, and this distracts me and suddenly out of nowhere there is a little pop, a breaking out of what is, indeed, a fart.

IT WASN'T A FOREBODING

The morning I left the Mayo, I had not even remotely pooped and the farts seemed faux and untrustworthy. I was starving and no one gave me food restrictions. Toast, Lu, and I were so excited to be off the Fart Floor to be in the sun, sitting outside at a restaurant, that we all ordered the special—there was something about the idea of special—eggs and pancakes. It felt perfectly midwestern and normal. I ate almost everything and fast. The idea was that I would stay at the Marriott for a few days until I pooped, then we would fly back to New York. After the special, I left Toast and Lu and crawled into bed. I was feeling a little queasy. I woke crawling on the floor, vomiting in a garbage pail. Whatever was supposed to be happening post-takedown, with the inversion of my stoma, in the now-healed pathway of my colon with my handsomedoctormade rectum was not happening. The nurses kept assuring me it took time for the body to relearn things. But my body had gone into a violent regression. There had been too much meddling, rearranging, removal, reversal, drilling, and reconstruction. The pancakes had begun to take possession like a dead animal drenched in maple syrup. I missed my bag. I needed my stoma. My body did not seem to remember how to defecate on its own. I was toxic and imploding. I vomited and vomited. I could not stop. It was as if something much deeper than the pancakes was trying to get out. They tried every antinausea drug and nothing prevented the retchingpurgingvomiting, the blood-bile sea of violence that washed through my veins and cells. It went on for three days. My body ached from retching. They gave me Marinol, chemical pot, and it made me raw and drastically depressed, and as I vomited, I hallucinated throwing up goldfish and pennies and chalk, but the puking did not stop. I puked out the absence, the lining of my gut and the insides of my organs and heart, I puked out the corneas of my eyes and terrible thoughts. The puking went on as the doctors came and whispered and the nurses stood by the bed, sometimes holding me, sometimes cleaning up. Toast and Lu huddled or paced or rocked with me. I was puking to death. My body ejecting itself. Retch, expel, get out. Get this out, out. There was something to get out. It was as if the whole journey of the last seven months had led me here. To a feeling, a memory, an image. As if through the journey of my body, through the excavating of organs and cancer, through the loss of weight from infection, through the evisceration of cells, and now through days of retching, the interior brush had been cleared and there was nothing covering or hiding the horror. I was at ground zero, back at the moment when I wanted no more of this world, back at the moment of witnessing what had shattered my psyche. Angelique in an exam room in Bukavu, telling me her story and then suddenly overcome with it, crawling on the floor, on the ground, pushing imaginary soldiers away, sealing her mouth, turning her head, screaming out as she sees again the pregnant womb of her best friend sliced wide open by a soldier and a half-formed baby tumbling out. The baby not ready for light or air or germs or loud raping men in uniforms. The umbilical cord still dangling, still attached to the mother bleeding all over the Congolese soil, the mother whose baby was severed from the cord and then tossed in the air like a ball by soldiers, the baby too embryonic to indicate pain, unable to cry or scream out, in front of the women, mothers whose babies had already been taken or murdered or strangled or dropped in the forest. Then the soldiers tossing the baby into a boiling pot, one of them with a knife, jabbing at the boiling flesh, raising it from the pot and shoving it at the women, scorching their mouths. Eat the baby or die. Eat the baby or have your head blown off. Angelique on the ground in the midst of a flashback, spitting, choking, scrambling, trying even now to get the horrible taste out of her mouth.

It was here I walked out of the world. Here in the forest, in the room on the floor, on the dirt with the woman screaming, begging, the woman crawling and crying out. Here where I decided to exit, to go, to check out. Here in the suspended somnolent zone where I told my body it was time to die. It was not a foreboding, as I thought. It was in fact a longing, a decision I made. How could I live when centuries of oppression and injustice had metastasized into this army of psychotic numbness and rage? How could I live with unborn babies and my faith in humanity gone? Now in my hotel room, I vomited and vomited and I saw how death had been my only comfort. I had quietly and secretly been moving toward it.

I decided early on as a child to make up the world. But on the day that Angelique crawled on the floor, my will and imagination collapsed. If humans were capable of this, if the superpowers were able to send militia proxies to do their bidding and steal the Congo's minerals, if the international community was able to turn a blind eye for thirteen years and eight million people were dead and hundreds of thousands of women raped and tortured and babies were cooked in pots, then all of us, every single one of us, was complicit and we were bankrupt and hopeless. I fell through this hole, this fistulaed crack in the world.

Cancer is essentially built into our DNA, our self-destruction programmed into our original design—biologically, psychologically. We spend our days, most of us consciously or unconsciously doing ourselves in. Think building a nuclear power plant on a fault line close to the water. Think poisoning the Earth that feeds us, the air that lets us breathe. Think smoking, drugging. Think abusing our children who are meant to care for us in old age, think mass raping women who carry the future in their bodies, think overeating or starving ourselves to look a certain way, think unprotected sex in the age of AIDS. We are a suicidal lot, propelled toward self-eradication. And now, they were putting a tube in through my nose, down my throat, into my gut, as if I had poisoned myself.

In the middle of this, Dr. Deb walked in.

I sat up and grabbed her arm hard, as if I had suddenly woken from a dream, and through my tube-filled nose and mouth I heard myself scream, "I want to live, Deb. I want to live. I don't want to die."

CONGO INCONTINENT

Three weeks after the takedown surgery and the removal of the bag, I return to the Congo. I am basically incontinent. I need the women. I need the jasmine and hibiscus and the howling night dogs and the mad rain and the lake that is an ocean and sometimes turns a certain moon blue. I need the South Kivu heat that surrounds and calms. I need the bougainvillea and the shocking orange blossoms on the tall trees. I need the bulging mangoes and avocados. I need to be woken by boisterous zebra finches, the colibri, moineaux—the chattering chorus of ancient morning birds. I need the incantations of women and men in the distance with drums summoning celebration or loss.

I return with my doctors: Dr. Sean and Dr. Deb from the Mayo. Dr. Sean, who removed my uterus and discovered my fistula, has to my astonishment and joy, offered to come to the Congo and perform surgery on women at Panzi Hospital, and Dr. Deb will advise and give support. They have brought tons of medical equipment. They are an entourage of love and healing. I return bald and twenty pounds thinner. The women do not know what to make of me. My naked head suddenly feels like insane privilege—all the attention and care I have received. I am embarrassed by how much money (insurance), equipment, healers, surgeons, nurses, and medications have gone into saving me.

These are the women who have been praying for me. When the women builders of City of Joy see me, they dance in the rain and mud. I dance with them. City of Joy is not finished.

Mama C is exhausted and we spend most of our days raging and worrying, but laughing a lot and singing along to blaring tragic love songs by Leona Lewis as we drive on what are euphemistically called roads.

One night after everyone has gone to bed, Dr. Sean and I end up talking. The night air relaxes me and gives me courage. This is the man who saved my life. This is also the man who scared me with his straightforwardness. He explains to me that he meant no harm, that he was only doing his job, laying out my options. I see how we have each been wounded in our various wars: Dr. Sean fighting on the front lines of cancer, me fighting on the front lines of sexual violence. He protects himself by preparing for the worst. I protect myself by not allowing space for it. I ask Dr. Sean what would happen if he were to let himself believe I was going to live. He says, "I am a doctor. It is about the science." I press him again. He finally says, "Honestly, Eve. I have no idea why I've become so cynical. Maybe it is all the cancer, the recurrences, the losses I have seen." His sorrow enters me. All the times he feels he has failed. He does not want to disappoint by promising what he cannot guarantee.

"There are no guarantees, Dr. Sean, but I would rather live on the mad edge of belief than shrink away, anticipating my doom. And right now," I say, "I need you to take a leap off the doctor cliff and believe with me." I am suddenly about seven years old. Dr. Sean is about five. We are in my backyard under my favorite weeping willow tree. I tell him if he closes his eyes and squeezes them really hard, he will see magical fairies. He says, in a frustrated voice, "I only see spots." "Squeeze harder, Dr. Sean," I say. "You will see them if you squeeze your eyes harder."

LEAKING

I go to visit Esther, Mama of the wounded at Panzi Hospital. We do our ritual together with hundreds of the women survivors. We breathe, scream, kick, punch, release, and then there is mad drumming and we dance. I am still weak from the takedown and chemo, but it doesn't stop me. As I dance, I have no control over my bowels, and for the first time I don't care. Before when I was with the women and *they* were leaking from their fistulas, I could only imagine what it felt like. Now we are one wild mass of drumming, kicking, raging, leaking women.

SHE WILL LIVE

Dr. Mukwege and I often visit his favorite places. We
have been to the top of the hills that overlook all of
Bukavu; there is one beaten, narrow footpath that
weaves like a snake through the lush fields. There the
air is soft and the Earth is fecund. We have walked in
the forests behind Panzi Hospital where the late-day
light filters through emerald trees and falls on a soft
carpet of pine needles and brush. We have walked for
hours through the back roads of the village of Panzi,
down by the river. Everywhere we go, Dr. Mukwege
stops to shake a hand or offer a remedy, or calm a heart.
He is the mayor, the pastor, the doctor, the healer. He
knows almost everyone's names and remembers each
of their maladies, stories, and treatments. Dr. Mukwege
is the antidote to my father. He is humble, quiet, careful, methodical. He listens. His story is in his hands,

large, capable, gentle, strong. Sometimes the magnitude and weight of what he has witnessed and experienced lies like a blanket of extended silence between us.

Today we drive for four hours to Kaziba, the village where his father was born. We drive on windy roads, through small dusty villages, past feeding goats and women who light up the road like fireflies in their brightly colored panges. From time to time I notice Dr. Mukwege checking me out, trying to assess if I am really well, if I am going to survive. It is seven months since I last saw him, since I was first diagnosed. I have lost my organs and my mother, and he has lost his father, who died last month. We arrive in the small backyard of his father's house where his father's body is buried. The markings are fresh. There is so much death in the Congo. I am suddenly aware of the new earth tossed over his coffin. I could easily be under that ground. I wonder where I would be buried or if I would be buried at all. I wish I had a village to return to. I dream sometimes of a plot in the Cimetière du Montparnasse in Paris, where Beauvoir and Sartre are buried, but here, in the backyard of Dr. Mukwege's father, that feels seriously pretentious. If I had my wish, they would take my body out to sea, gently lower it in the waves, and let the sharks and whales and other fish feed on it.

I don't mind the idea of being left in water. I begin to have the "death thing," but I notice it is not scary like it used to be. I have already come so close, the proximity has changed my relationship to death, and my gratitude for being alive provides a new protection. I am lost in these musings when Dr. Mukwege says quietly but decisively, "I want to tell you something." As you know, my father was a pastor," he says, "and he knew things. In 2000, he came to the family and said, 'I will leave this world in ten years on October 7, 2010. I have received a message from God.' For ten years on October 7, we had a family celebration of the day of his passing. In fact, he died on October 7. It was strange that it happened during your last operation, but there are so many strange things about our connection. When I heard you were sick, I got very depressed. I couldn't understand how God could take you away when you had come to help us. I was in a bad place. My father could see I was not well. My faith was in question. He came to me and said, 'Denis, listen to me. Your friend Eve is sick. She will go through a rough time, but she will not die. The cancer will pass and she will be fine. You do not have to worry. God is protecting her.'"

Dr. Mukwege says, "I did not fully believe him, but when I see you, when I see how strong you are, I know

now he was telling the truth." For the very first time in seven months, something unhinges inside me and I sense the future. As we drive back to Bukavu through the melting green countryside, I am not sure if it is the jeep or my newborn faith propelling us forward.

SUE

Sue: "I am imagining you writing, looking out a window, with snow falling, quiet—your heart and creativity safe, sheltered, expanding.

"I cherish our bond, always, and I can feel how much your joy has grown, and how much it is the great force behind your work now. Amazing how cancer could transform you like this, isn't it?

"Wouldn't it be incredible if everyone could be purged, somehow, of the projected not-them badness that they internalized and perhaps have acted out because their souls have been so damaged?

"Wouldn't it be incredible if everyone could find the joy that comes with committing to our own goodness? Perhaps we would stop dividing ourselves into malignancies of various forms."

JOY

My hair is cropped. My body is lean, dressed in a special Congolese-designed short skirt and geometric top. It is Western enough to prevent me from looking like a tragic white-wannabe-African but Congolese enough to be respectful. It is colorful. I am trying not to wear only black. Dr. Mukwege and Mama C and I stand at the entranceway and greet the thousands of guests who are arriving for the opening of City of Joy. There are dignitaries who have come from all over the Congo and the world, government and UN officials, the governor of South Kivu, ambassadors and their wives; there are famous actors and funders, and my dear friends Pat, Carole, Rada, Naomi, Avi, Katharine, and Stephen, my team at V-Day, and our amazing board. Paula is taking photographs. Toast is here. There are thousands from the surrounding community: pastors, doctors, nurses, and social workers. There are ministers and teachers, mothers and fathers, and babies. My son has flown here. When he walks through the gates, I start to cry.

I stand at the entranceway of a vision that propelled me through surgery and infections and chemo and rock-bottom worry and despair.

City of Joy is a place, but it is also a concept. It grew out of the women of the Congo and it was shaped by their desire and hunger. It was literally built with their hands. It is a sanctuary for healing; it is a revolutionary center. It is a place where on any given day women will learn English, literacy skills, self-defense, computer skills, agricultural techniques, communications, and civics. They will spend mornings singing and dancing and healing in group psychotherapy, and end the day with massages and cooking together. Their healing is entwined with their empowerment so that when they leave City of Joy after six months, they will be leaders who teach their communities what they have learned. Through the dissemination of their skills and training, a network of Congolese women leaders will spread and Cities of Joy will grow everywhere.

There will be joy here. Joy—happiness, delight, plea-sure, bliss, ecstasy, elation, thrill, exultation, rapture. This joy will be palpable when you walk through the gates. It will be found in the green grass, in the voices of the women, in the taste of their home-cooked cassava, sweet potatoes, fufu, and peas, in their grateful bodies dancing and dancing to what will feel like a ceaseless drum. It will move through you and you will touch joy and suddenly realize you have never felt joy because it requires abandon. It grows from gratitude and cannot exist where there is mad cynicism or distrust. You will touch this joy and you will suddenly know it is what you were looking for your whole life, but you were afraid to even acknowledge the absence because the hunger for it was so encompassing.

I am standing at the entranceway of the new city. I am still thin and weak. My body is not yet fully mine, in the last stages of this cancer conversion. I am not sure who I will be when all this is over or where I will live or even what I will want to do with my life. But I know for sure that there will be joy.

MOTHER

I have never gone to see the gorillas. I have never felt comfortable being a tourist in the middle of a raging war. I have said I will go when the women are free and safe. The day after the opening of City of Joy, it suddenly feels right. I will take my son. He will love the gorillas. We drive with Mama C's husband, Carlos, and son, David, up to the national park. We are told to wear high boots and socks so the red stinging ants do not attack our ankles. We are told this is agony. We are told we will go into the forest and walk until we find the gorillas. We are told it could happen right away or it could take hours. I am not sure what I am more afraid of—ants, or snakes, or spiders, or getting lost in the thick jungle and being captured by raping militias. I do not want my son to be afraid, so I turn my terror into enthusiasm. I am dancing and leaping over rocks and vines and roots. Dancing through the forest. Part of it is a strategy to avoid crawling things or leeches. We have two Congolese guides who carry huge machetes and chop at the vines and trees to make a path. They thrash and thrash at wet leaves as we move deeper and deeper into the jungle. Serious jungle. This is the Earth, raw, untended, untamed. This is the Mother before makeup, dieting, cutting, and pruning. The earthy smell of wet soil, the green oxygen of trees, the solid dirt floor. I can tell that my son, who lives in Brentwood, is trying to manage his terror. His jokes get funnier and more inappropriate.

This is a fairy tale. The handsome prince who lost his mother to an evil killer gets taken by the wild stepmother into the woods to see if they can find the secret that will set them free. As they step deeper and deeper into the tangled woods, part of them would like to turn back, but something drives them farther. After a while they stop talking. The cacophony of the forest— the overworked woodpeckers, the croaking frogs, the incessant cicadas—fills their beings. Maybe an hour in, their guides suddenly come to an abrupt halt. The handsome prince and the wild stepmother cling to each other. The guides motion them to hush, and they slowly climb a hill, gently pushing back the trees with hands, no longer using their machetes. They all tiptoe until they come upon a small clearing. Their guides, smiling and proud, motion the handsome prince and the wild stepmother to come closer. There in the middle of the forest, in the middle of an ordinary day, is a family of totally happy gorillas: the ancient sleeping grandfather, snoring and scratching; the teenager, like an acrobat from the tree circus, swinging from vines above; the mother sitting crossed-legged on the ground, her newborn to her breast, making the simplest and most earth-shattering gesture. When she sees the approaching invaders, the crowd of seekers, she simply, calmly, without thought or hesitation, closes her arms around her baby. The prince and the stepmother are stunned. It is this simple gesture they have each been searching for all their lives—the arms of the mother who instinctively and absolutely protects her vulnerable baby. The handsome prince and the wild stepmother, two orphans, gripping each other's hands a little too hard.

SECOND WIND

Live as if you were already dead.
Zen admonition

I am on Essence Road. It is after the rain.

I am cancer-free eighteen months.

I know the crisis on Essence Road in Bukavu is the crisis in the world. Indigenous people starving as their government exports their crops. Indigenous people making a dollar or two a day (if they are lucky) as the West and the world pillage their plentiful oil, gold, copper, coltain, or tin. Women carrying insane loads, sacks, tanks, baskets. Women putting their lives at risk, and getting raped.

Each time I take this journey, I force myself to look out at Essence Road, to pay attention to the details, to map the changes and outrages, insults and miseries. I do not look away, and, believe me, I want to look away. It's hot on Essence Road. It's crowded and it's impossible. Most of the people here have fled violence. Nearly everyone has left their homes. Most are traumatized, dislocated, orphaned, hungry. Essence Road burns in me and I would be lying if I didn't tell you that some days when I consider why Essence Road and so many roads like it exist all over the world, I have very violent fantasies. I think of rapacious greed, the hunger for more and more, the tiny percentage of those who have everything, and the majority who have nothing. In my rage, I imagine the overthrow of corporations, industrial destroyers, rapists, corrupt leaders, and the arrogant and disinterested rich. Some days I think there will be no other way. None of the powers that be will voluntarily give up their private holdings and their dreams. I try to explain to myself how I can be having such murderous fantasies about uprising and revolution when I have spent my life devoted to ending violence. And the only answer I can find is also on Essence Road—the City of Joy. Each time I arrive there, I am reminded again that we can build the new way, build the new world, birth the new paradigm.

I do not know how to end the war in the Democratic Republic of the Congo. I don't know where governments end and corporations begin. I cannot show you exactly how the mining of the coltain that is in your cell phone is linked to Jeanne being raped in her village. I don't know how to move the UN Security Council, or the secretary-general, or the European, British, or Canadian Parliament, or Congress or Downing Street or the White House, and I have made impassioned visits to all these places and have left each time, crushed and bewildered. I do not know how to arrest the war criminals or the corporate exploiters.

I do know that the minute I enter the City of Joy everything seems possible. It is green and clean. It is the lotus rising from the mud. It is the metaphor for a new beginning, for building a new world.

Three of the ten principles governing the City of Joy are (a) tell the truth, (b) stop waiting to be rescued, and (c) give away what you want the most.

In the City of Joy I know how to do things: how to hug Telusia, Jeanne, and Prudence, and how to remind them not to turn their gaze away because the shame they carry is not their own. I know how to listen and how to keep asking questions.

I know how to cry and that if I love the women of the Congo, and I don't close off my heart, that love will cut a path, a plan will be revealed, and I will find the money and everything that is necessary. Because love does that.

Having cancer was the moment when I went as far as I could go without being gone, and it was there, dangling on that edge, that I was forced to let go of everything that didn't matter, to release the past and be burned down to essential matter. It was there I found my second wind. The second wind arrives when we think we are finished, when we can't take another step, breathe another breath. And then we do.

Because City of Joy is in a valley, the air is always fresh. Sometimes late in the day, after the singing of the women has died down, a wind comes, a delicious, clean wind. I believe in wind. It pollinates and moves things around. It can cool us off. It can make electricity. It can scatter seeds. It can become a hurricane or a tornado or typhoon. It can rustle the leaves. It rises up and it can help us rise up too.

What does it mean to have a second wind, a second life? It means screaming *fire* when there is a fire. It means touching the darkness and entering it and tasting death in the earthquake scar down the center of my torso, in the first scan that announces the chances are good it's in my liver. I am burning because the second wind is also a fire that will burn through our fear. We cannot be afraid of anything, not of anything. There is no one coming but us.

The second wind is not about having or getting or buying or acquisition. It is about giving everything up,

giving more than you thought you owned, giving dou-
ble what you are taking. What is coming is not like
anything we have ever known before. Your dying, my
dying is necessary and irrelevant and inevitable. Do
not be afraid, no, death will not be our end. Indifference will be, disassociation will be, collateral damage,
polar caps melting, endless hunger, mass rapes, grotesque wealth. The change will come from those who
know they do not exist separately but as part of the
river. If you want to overcome your sickness, reach out
to someone who is sick. If you want to forget your hunger, feed your friend. You worry about germs and
stockpile your herbs, but they will not save you, nor
will your fancy house or gated villages. The only salva-
tion is kindness. The only way out is care. The second
wind will come from the ground, the Earth. It will rise
like a dust storm. It will suddenly appear from the corners and the barrios, the favelas and the invisible places
where most of the world lives. Because the streets are
alive, and the women who carry the two-hundred-
pound sacks are alive, and they dance. The second wind
will be brought by the girls. By the girls. By the girls. It
is in them and of them. This wind will take everything
away. And those of you who can live without will survive. Those of you who can be naked, without a bank
account, a known future, or even a place to call home.
Those of you who can live without and find your mean-

ing here, here, wherever here is. Knowing the only des-
tination is change. The only port is where we are going.
The second wind may take what you think you need or
want the most, and what you lost and how you lost it
will determine if you survive.

I have lost my organs and at times my mind. I know it is
a race now between the people who are helping themselves to the Earth, to the loot, and the rest of us. I
despise charity. It gives crumbs to a few and silences the
others. Either we go all the way now or there is no more
way. Who will step off the wheel? Who will join the
women who have lived in the forests, in the projects, in
the loud and cramped cities and who carry sacks of pain
on their backs and hungry babies on their breasts, who
are not counted, but whose strength and whose work
hold up the world? Who will stand with them and trust
that they have always known the way? The world burns
in my veins, just like chemo did only a few months ago.
I dare you to stop counting and start acting. To stop
pleasing and start defying. I dare you to trust what you
know. The second wind is beyond data. It is past pain. It
is found in the bloodstream and cells of the women and
men who purged the poison of their perpetrators, who
walked through the cancer, the nightmares. The second
wind is coming from your body, it's in your mouth, it's
in the way you move your hips.

Every vision is necessary now. Every instinct must be awakened. The wind does not turn away. It blows through everything. Do not be afraid. There is no more winning and losing. We have already lost. Even the so-called winners feel that way. That is why they can't stop self-destructing. Step off the wheel of winning and losing. Of course there is risk. Of course it is dangerous. I wish I could make this easy for you. I wish I could tell you there is nothing to lose. Lose everything. That is where it begins. Each one of you will know in what direction you need to move and who to take with you. You will recognize the others when you arrive. Build the circles. Listen to the voice inside. And when they come and say, "This is the one way only some can profit, we need the oil, we need the drilling, the reactors, the tar sands, the fracking, the coltain, the coal," stay tight in your circle. Dance in the circles. Sing in the circles. Join arms in the circles. Surrender your comfort. We must be willing to go the distance. We must be willing to leave the kingdom and surrender the treasures.

We are the people of the second wind. We, who have been undermined, reduced, and minimized, we know who we are. Let us be taken. Let us turn our pain to power, our victimhood to fire, our self-hatred to action, our self-obsession to service, to fire, to wind. Wind.

Wind. Be transparent as wind, be as possible and relentless and dangerous, be what moves things forward without needing to leave a mark, be part of this collection of molecules that begins somewhere unknown and can't help but keep rising. Rising. Rising. Rising

ACKNOWLEDGMENTS

Thank you to Charlotte Sheedy, who has been in my corner and my heart for almost forty years—thank you for listening to these pages and believing early.

To Frances Coady, who edited this book with the care, devotion, and craft of a surgeon and who gave me courage.

To Sara Bershtel and everyone at Metropolitan for believing in this book with their whole hearts.

To the circle of friends and family who visited and loved me back to life: Pat Mitchell, Carole Black, James Lescene, Paula Allen, Kim Rosen, Olivier Mevel, Diana de Vegh, Mark Matousek, Katherine Ensler, Adisa Krupalija, David Rivel, Hannah Ensler-Rivel, Jane Fonda, Denis Mukwege, Christine Shuler Descryver, Laura

Flanders and Elizabeth Streb, Naomi Klein and Avi Lewis, Stephen Lewis, Amy Goodman, Rada Boric, Nicoletta Billi, Marie Cecile Renauld, Marie Astrid Perimony and Alexia Perimony, Donna Karan, Cari Ross, Emily Scott Pottruck, Jennifer Buffett, Beth Dozoretz, Mellody Hobson, Katherine McFate, Linda Pope, Amy Rao, Sheryl Sandberg, Lisa Schejola Akin, Jodie Evans, Elizabeth Lesser, Andrew Harvey, Curtis Ensler, Nancy Rose, George Lane, David Stone, Frank Selvaggi, Kerry Washington, Rosario Dawson, Glenn Close, Purva Panday Cullman, Susan Celia Swan, Cecile Lipworth, Harriet Clark, Monique Wilson, Urvashi Vaid, Shiva Rose, Brenda Currin and Marie Howe.

To all the doctors and healers who literally saved my life and put me back together: Dr. Louis Katz, Dr. Deb Rhodes, Dr. Sean Dowdy, Dr. Eric Dozois, Dr. Ilan Shapira, Dr. John Koulos, Dr. Joseph Martz.

The nurses at the Mayo Clinic, especially Sara, Rhonda and Monica, and the nurses at Beth Israel, especially Elizabeth, Regina, and Diane.

The women who healed and protected my body at its most vulnerable time—Maryanne Travaligone, Ruth Pontvianne, Deirdre Hade, Maryann Savarice.

Bassia—whose delicious cooking kept my appetite alive.

My extraordinary V-day team, who stepped in and moved it all forward—Carl Cheng, Kate Fisher, Shael Norris, Nikki Noto, Amy Squires, Laura Waleryszak.

All the friends, activists, family who sent me prayers, gifts, emails, flowers, and cards.

My son, Dylan McDermott; my granddaughters, Coco and Charlotte McDermott—my family, my heart.

Tony Montenieri and Laura Ensler, who were there every day with cool washcloths, irony, pills, and courage.

The women of the Congo—you are my strength and my reason.

EVE ENSLER is an internationally bestselling author and an award-winning playwright whose theatrical works include *The Vagina Monologues*, *Necessary Targets*, and *The Good Body*. She is the author of *Insecure at Last*, a political memoir, and *I Am an Emotional Creature*, a *New York Times* bestseller, which she has since adapted for the stage as *Emotional Creature*. Ensler is the founder of V-Day, the global movement to end violence against women and girls, which has raised over $90 million for local groups and activists and inspired the global action "One Billion Rising." Eve Ensler lives in the world.